CU00694686

ARI SCHONBRUN

miracles
& fate
on 78

A 9/11 Story of Inspiration

ARI SCHONBRUN

miracles
& fate
on 78

A 9/11 Story of Inspiration

FIRST EDITION
Designed by James Iacobelli

Library of Congress Cataloging-in-Publication Data

Schonbrun, Ari

Miracles & Fate on 78: A 9/11 Story of Inspiration / by Ari Schonbrun

p. cm.

ISBN 978-0-615-53403-9

$17.99

1. Ari Schonbrun 2. Autobiography I. Title

09 10 11 12 13   OV/RRD   10 9 8 7 6 5 4 3 2 1

This book is dedicated to my family, who gave me strength to go on after the tragedy.

To the 658 of my friends and coworkers at Cantor Fitzgerald who perished.

To all the victims who lost their lives on that day.

And last, but not least, to Virginia.

May the words of Isaiah come true speedily in our day:

They will beat their swords into plowshares
and their spears into pruning hooks.

Nation will not take up sword against nation,
nor will they train for war anymore.

ARI SCHONBRUN

ACKNOWLEDGMENTS

It took me a very long time to write this book. Although the writing itself only took about nine months, the decision to write the book took nine years. When I first started speaking about my 9/11 experience people were fascinated and always asked me if I had written a book. My answer was always the same: I am a speaker, not a writer. After many years of people asking me if they could buy my book, I decided that it might be something that I should do. My very first attempt was to listen to one of my talks and just write down exactly what I had said. When I finished doing that, I realized how awful it was and decided that I was not going to write a book. Several years after that, when my speaking career had really started to take off, I was told that if I really wanted to take my speaking to the next level, I would have to write a book. I remembered the first time I tried that so this time I decided that I was going to get a ghost writer to help me write the book. The first person whom I had hired didn't work out. Our styles were too different, and the book just wasn't going in the direction that I wanted it to go in. The second person was all gung ho, but she was just in the middle of something and promised to get back to me in a few weeks. Three months had gone by and I had not heard from her so I passed on that one. Then I was talking to my uncle's brother and asked if he would be interested since he had just retired and he had published in the educational field. He told me that he couldn't commit, but his daughter, Lisa, was an excellent writer and I should speak to her. She hadn't written a book, but she had written many articles and her writing was good. I met with her for hours, and she agreed to do the book. After about six weeks, I had not heard from her, and when I finally called her she told me that being a single mom with two little girls at home, holding down a full-time job, she just didn't have the time to commit to the project. Here I was back at square one. So I asked her, "If I write the book, will you edit it"? That she agreed to do. So I started to write from my heart and sent her chapters at a time via e-mail. Believe it or not, it worked. A problem arose as I was finishing the book. I realized that I wasn't sure why I was writing the book in the first place. Just because people told me to write a book was not a great reason to write it. I needed to dig deep down and figure out why. What was my message? What did I want to accomplish by writing this book? I realized that I had no idea. So I decided to go back and speak to some ghost writers for their opinion about the book. Everybody loved it, but it was a work in progress without an end. I still needed to figure out the end. I was very frustrated and decided to scrap the whole idea. Then I went on a weekend retreat in Stamford, Connecticut. It was a weekend where Jews from all walks of life gathered together in a show of unity. It was called "One Shabbos." I was there because I had been asked to deliver the keynote speech on Sunday morning to wrap up the weekend. I remember listening to speaker after speaker and I was inspired. Then I met Charlie Harary. He became my hero. He was the most dynamic speaker I had ever heard. I was mesmerized the whole weekend. We became friendly, and when he found out that I was the one delivering the keynote on Sunday, he was very excited. I told him not to get too excited. I did not feel that I was up to his level. Sunday rolled around and I gave my talk. Charlie came up to me after my talk and told me that he was speechless. He told me it was the most inspiring story he had ever heard. "You have to write a book," he told me. "I can't," I replied. "I've tried but I can't. It's too short, I don't have an ending, nobody is going to want it." It was at that moment that he said to me, "Forget about everybody else. Forget about how long or short it is. Forget about everything. If you can put it on paper the way you put it out to the audience… from your heart, that's all you need. Just do it." And that is when I decided to resume writing the book, and this time I vowed to finish it.

Once it was done I needed to have it edited, but I was out of time. Or so I thought. In steps Alan

Rubin. I met Alan three years ago when I went to Israel with my son Avrumi for his Bar Mitzvah. We went on a mission to help an orphanage named Migdal Ohr. And Alan was on that trip. We spent a wonderful week together and became friends but he lived in Florida and I lived in New York and so I didn't think I would ever see him again. We just didn't travel in the same circles. Fast forward three years and I get a call from Alan. He is moving to New York and would love to see me. When we got together and I told him about my project he was so excited that he jumped right in. He had many connections and hooked me up with an editor. He has been guiding me every step of the way and promised that he will be with me until this project gets done.

So, first and foremost, I would like to thank Lisa Stiskin Melman, without whom the project would not have gotten off the ground in the first place. Your editing and urging gave me the strength to continue even when I wanted to quit.

Next I would like to thank Adam Wildstein and all of my friends at Aish, New York, who kept telling me that I could do this. Adam worked with me in trying to decide ghost writers (yes or no), publishers, editors, etc. He too was just one of those people who kept telling me "you can do it."

Of course, I must thank Charlie Harary, who was the ultimate driver at the very end when I had given up. The funny thing is, he doesn't even know it and he won't know it until he reads this.

Next is my friend Alan. He has been my right hand man and I can tell you without a shadow of a doubt that if he had not come onto the scene, this book would never have happened. Thank you Alan. May God bless you forever and ever.

Last but not least, I have to thank my wife, Joyce. She understood how important this work was and gave me the space to do it when I needed to. There were times when things were crazy in the house, but if she saw me working on the manuscript, she would always leave me be and tend to everything that was going on in the house. She is a true woman of valor and I thank God everyday that He gave her to me. May God watch over you all of your days.

HISTORY OF THE WORLD TRADE CENTER

01 The World Trade Center (WTC) opened in 1970 after
eight years of construction.

02 The WTC was the dream of David Rockefeller, chair-
man of the Chase Manhattan Bank, and Nelson
Rockefeller, former governor of New York.

03 The Rockefellers wanted to name the towers after
themselves, but the mayor of New York, John Lindsay,
insisted on calling it the World Trade Center.

04 The city chose to build the WTC instead of building a
new tunnel and large bridge over the Hudson River.

05 The World Trade Center was designed by architect
Minora Yamasaki.

06 According to Yamasaki, downtown Manhattan was
the perfect place to erect the towers because
there wasn't "a single building worth saving in the
neighborhood."

07 Owners of nearby buildings disagreed and delayed
   demolition by three weeks with their protests.

08 Sixteen blocks were cleared to house the completed WTC.

09 More than 10,000 workers were involved in building
   the complex.

10 More than sixty workers died during construction of
   the WTC.

11 The excavation work displaced enough soil to create
   Liberty Park, where four sixty-floor towers and four
   apartment buildings were constructed.

12 The WTC's foundations were laid at 60 feet below
   ground level.

13 The complex covered 16 acres when finished.

14 In addition to the towers, five other office buildings
   made up the WTC complex.

15 The WTC had 12 million square feet of space.

16 Each floor was 50,000 square feet.

17 The buildings had their own ZIP codes: 10047 and 10048.

18 The towers were designed to look like a futuristic sculpture.

19 The structure was revolutionary. Its main supports were external, lining the four corners of each tower.

20 Critics condemned the completed buildings as "boring."

21 The towers were 100 feet taller than the Empire State Building.

22 Until the construction of Chicago's Sears Tower and the Petronas Towers in Kuala Lumpur, Malaysia, the twin towers were the world's tallest buildings.

23 Even after the construction of the Sears Tower and the Petronas Towers, the North Tower's 347-foot radio tower meant that technically, it was still the world's tallest building.

24 The towers were different heights. The South Tower
    was 1,362 feet tall, and big brother North Tower was
    1,368 feet tall.

25 Sixty-eight miles of steel were used in the construc-
    tion of the buildings.

26 The concrete poured was enough to build a road from
    New York to Washington, D.C.

27 The steel inside the WTC could have made three more
    Brooklyn Bridges.

28 The Twin Towers had more than 16 miles of staircases.

29 There were 43,600 windows in the Twin Towers.

30 The windows were small to reduce the heat or cold
    entering the building. Regular-sized windows would
    have made the heat unbearable in the summertime.

31 The WTC's 600,000 square feet of glass was cleaned by
    an automatic machine.

32 The buildings had 20,000 elevator doors.

33 Of the WTC's 239 banks of elevators, one was known
    as the fastest in the United States.

34 The main elevators, which traveled at 27 feet per
    second, reached the top in less than a minute.

35 There were 828 emergency exit doors in the towers.

36 A total of 23,000 fluorescent light bulbs lit the interiors
    of the towers.

37 Originally, there were no light switches in the towers
    because energy prices were one-third less than they
    are today. In 1982, switches were installed.

38 A total of 12,000 miles of electrical cable snaked through
    the buildings, supplying power to fifteen trading floors
    for stockbrokers.

39 The 75,000 telephones in the towers were maintained
    by 19,600 miles of cable.

40 There were more than 300 computer mainframes on site.

41 The WTC used more power in one day than most small
    American cities.

42 Steam supplied by a plant on New York's East River
    was used to heat the buildings.

43 The buildings housed 49,000 tons of air-conditioning
    equipment.

44 More than 250,000 cans of paint were needed every
    year for upkeep of the towers.

45 The surrounding shopping center complex included
    325,000 square feet of restaurants and stores.

46 Six banks, five investment firms and three insurance
    companies had their headquarters in the towers.

47 The Port Authority of New York and New Jersey had its
    headquarters in the towers.

48 American Express had three floors in the WTC.

49 The WTC was home base for Bank of America.

50 The WTC housed two top restaurants—the Windows on the World and Wild Blue.

51 Windows on the World had one of the best vintage wine collections in the United States.

52 More than 50,000 people worked in the Twin Towers.

53 By 9 a.m. each weekday morning, the buildings had an average of 35,000 employees at their desks.

54 More than 200,000 people—half of them tourists—moved through the buildings each day.

55 The South Tower had an observation deck that was visited by more than 26,000 people a day.

56 An information sign at the top assured visitors that the buildings had been designed to withstand airplane crashes.

57 The towers could be seen from at least 20 miles away.

58 On a clear day, it was possible to see for 45 miles in every direction from the observation deck.

59 The express elevator to the observation deck was the largest in the United States with a fifty-five-person capacity.

60 Every president since 1973 paid a visit to the landmark.

61 President Ronald Reagan watched July 4th fireworks celebrations from the WTC on two occasions.

62 Superstars Frank Sinatra, John Lennon, Mick Jagger and Liza Minnelli all sang in WTC restaurants.

63 Two New York TV stations incorporated the Twin Towers image into their logos.

64 The towers served ten New York TV stations with ten antennas on the top.

65 More postcards of the WTC were sent each year than
    any other building in the world.

66 In 1974, a Frenchman, Philippe Petit, strung a tight-
    rope between the two towers and walked across.

67 Three men successfully parachuted from the top of the
    towers.

68 More than a dozen mountain climbers have scaled the
    building.

69 In 1975 a jobless construction worker parachuted
    from the South Tower to publicize the plight of the
    unemployed.

70 The most famous man to climb the building was
    George Willig—he was arrested at the top.

71 Willig was fined one penny for each of the 110 floors he
    scaled.

72 A man in a micro-light aircraft crashed into the North Tower.

73 In the concourse beneath the towers, there were more than 75 stores.

74 Each day, over 150,000 commuters passed through the three subway stations there.

75 Eighty-seven tons of food were delivered to the buildings each day.

76 Over 30,000 cups of coffee were poured daily in the basement cafes.

77 Twenty-two doctors had practices on site.

78 Seventeen babies were born on site.

79 Larry Silverstein bought the WTC for almost $3.2 billion in July 2001.

80 The WTC generated $110 million a year in profit.

81 More than three dozen movies have been filmed there.

82 The best-known film to use the WTC as a location was the 1976 remake of *King Kong*.

83 The 1993 bombing of the WTC killed six people and injured 1,000 more.

84 In the 1993 attack, 1,300 pounds of explosives ripped through the garage.

85 The 1993 bombing created a crater 16 feet deep and badly damaged inner support beams.

86 Before the 1993 attack, there were three closed circuit television networks for security.

87 After the bombing, the number of cameras were increased to 300, monitored by computers.

88 More than 300 security guards worked on site.

89 The WTC featured security centers on fourteen different floors and its own police station.

90 The entrance lobbies had sixteen concierge desks and twelve X-ray machines.

91 After the 1993 bombing, no one could get inside the buildings without an ID check.

92 It took an average of five minutes for a visitor to pass through security checks.

93 Before the 1993 bombing, there were more than 1,000 parking spaces beneath the buildings; 600 remained afterward.

94 All vehicles using the parking lot had to show FBI security passes.

95 On September 11, the building was 95 percent full, with over 400 tenants.

96 New York Governor George Pataki had an office in the WTC, but he wasn't there when the disaster struck.

97 Both the Secret Service and the FBI rented office space in the WTC.

98 A total of $110.3 million in gold and $120.7 million in silver was buried in the rubble.

99 The combined weight of the towers was more than 1.5 million tons.

100 Each tower was built to safely sway about three feet during strong wind storms.

101 Blue Cross-Blue Shield, New York's largest health insurance company, moved into the building three years prior to 9/11.

102 Nine chapels serving six different faiths called the WTC home.

103 Twenty-nine countries had trade mission offices in the buildings.

104 Every major U.S. airline had ticket offices inside the WTC.

105 The towers were the first skyscrapers in the world destroyed by terrorists.

My name is Ari Schonbrun, and I work for a company by the name of Cantor Fitzgerald. This simple statement, which, prior to 9/11, used to be matter-of-fact, now causes people to stop in their tracks when I meet them.

On September 11, 2001, we occupied the top five floors—101 to 105—of One World Trade Center, otherwise known as the North Tower of the Twin Towers. Most people would simply think of it as the tower with the big antenna. At this location, our New York headquarters, we employed 1,000 people. On that September day, the following was the roll call that changed Cantor Fitzgerald, and myself, forever—658 employees were sitting at their desks, 1 employee was in the lobby of One World Trade, 2 employees were riding elevators on their way up to the upper floors, and 1 employee was on the 78th floor sky lobby about to get on an elevator to go up to the upper floors.

On that day, the 658 of my coworkers—many of whom were also my friends—who were sitting at their desks were brutally murdered simply because of where they happened to be at that fateful moment in time. The two employees in the elevator and the employee in the lobby were so severely burned that they spent months in hospitals, at times in induced comas. I was the one employee on the 78th floor in between elevators; and, against all odds, I somehow managed to escape without a single scratch. Somebody, obviously, was watching out for me that day.

Being in that exact spot, at that precise moment in time, allowed me to remain alive—and the experience of living against all odds has changed everything about who I am and how I move forward in my life. Like any survivor, I now see my life separated into three distinct parts: before, during and after.

before

ARI SCHONBRUN

CHAPTER 1

My early life was pretty typical of a Jewish Orthodox American kid growing up in New York during the sixties. My parents and extended family were very close. Not far removed from their immigrant past, they had moved closer toward achieving the American dream and were steadily increasing the quality of life for their children. Like any childhood, mine had its pleasurable times and its challenges; and these experiences molded me. Most of all, I learned how places and situations (even in times of peace) can be impermanent; how we have to adapt to the changes that force themselves upon us; how we need to persevere through all the ups and downs of life; and how we always must hope for the best outcome, no matter the challenges that may come your way.

The third of four children, I was born in 1957. Our family lived in an apartment in the Crown Heights section of Brooklyn, New York, until I was six years old. My sister was the oldest and then there were the three boys. I was the middle boy and always knew, and sometimes even said, that I suffered from middle child syndrome. My older brother often got his way because he was the oldest, and my young brother always got his way because he was, after all, the baby. I, on the other hand, inevitably got the short end of the stick. Or at least that's how it felt.

In 1963, when I was six years old, my parents bought a two-family house together with my aunt and uncle in the Bayswater section of Far Rockaway, New York. We were a typical middle-class family. My father was an insurance investigator, and in 1965, he went to work for himself. That same year, my uncle started a school for children with learning disabilities, and my mother joined him as a partner.

As Orthodox Jews steeped in our faith, we all were sent to the local yeshiva, where we received a religious education as well as a secular one.

When I was twelve, however, my family's life changed dramatically. My older brother, Moshe (he was Mark back then), went fishing in the bay a few blocks from our house. He absolutely loved to fish; and to this day, it remains a passion. But on that day while he was fishing, three black kids attacked him, beat him up, and stole his fishing rod. My parents reported it to the police, and a detective came to interview my brother and work on the case. The police ended up finding the boys who beat him up, but the detective told my parents that it didn't pay to press charges. He said there might be consequences and that we may not be safe from the families of these boys. This was not the society—or the place—in which my mother wanted to bring up her children.

My aunt and uncle were planning on moving to Israel the following year. My mother, who was very close to my aunt and with whom she had similar views, decided we would join them. Her plan was to move us there in two years, but my father wasn't too keen on the idea since he had just started doing very well with his new business. My sister, having finished a semester at Brooklyn College, decided that she would prefer to complete her education in Israel, and my brother, who had gone to Israel for a visit that summer, decided he didn't want to come home. Since he loved the country and wanted to stay, my parents found a school for him. He would live with my mother's uncle until we joined him.

That was the summer of 1969. In June of 1971, when it was time for the rest of the family to move, I was less than thrilled with the idea. I was fourteen years old and would be leaving all of my friends. My entire grade threw a surprise bowling party for me, and that just made it harder. I was not a happy camper.

But the decision had been made. I had to give up everything I knew and go on, and so I hoped for the best. When we got to Israel, we lived in an apartment complex in Herzelia. There was a pool in the complex, and we were a mile from the beach. It was a great summer. We either went down to the pool or to the beach every day. The only downer of that summer for me was the fact that I had to go to a tutor several times a week to learn geometry in Hebrew. I even met another American boy who was my age and we became good friends. As it turned out, we went to the same school. It was like going away on vacation, and it helped with the transition. When the following school year started, my parents sent me to an elite school that was an hour away from where we lived; so at the ripe old age of fourteen, I found myself living in a dorm with five other kids, all Israelis. Unfortunately, I couldn't speak Hebrew very well, and since they couldn't speak much English, communicating with them was a major problem. On top of the language barrier, they didn't really like Americans. They thought we were spoiled. And during those first few months, I got into many fights.

My academic situation wasn't much better. All the subjects were taught completely in Hebrew, with which I was still struggling. Despite having been a straight "A" student my whole life, during the first trimester of school in Israel, I actually failed all my classes except English and math. I remember crying to my parents that I wanted to go back to the States. My father told me that if I felt that way by the end of the year, he would send me back to New York, but I had to finish out the year. This was a smart move on my father's part. He knew that I would ultimately adapt, learn the language, make friends, and be fine. And that is exactly what happened.

In the fall of 1973, the Yom Kippur War broke out. It was a very scary time. I had never lived through a war. Nothing in my past as a typical American kid had prepared me for anything like it. Hearing air-raid sirens and fleeing into bomb shelters were my new reality. One of my school administrators was killed in the war; another faculty member had a mental breakdown. In times like that, kids grow up very quickly. Most people don't realize it, but Israel was on the verge of extinction. Golda Meir, who was then the Prime Minister of Israel, called Secretary of State Henry Kissinger and told him that if the United States did not come to their aid, she would be left with no choice but to launch a nuclear attack against Israel's enemies. She argued that the Arabs might destroy Israel, but their armies would have no countries—no homes—to go back to. Thankfully, the United States did send aid, and Israel ultimately won the war.

Eventually, circumstances took me away from my life in Israel. By the time I was done with Bar Ilan University, job prospects in Israel were not very good; so I made the decision to return to the States. After working in a few different fields, I decided to go into banking. In 1981, I got a job working for the UMB Bank and Trust Company, a subsidiary of United Mizrahi Bank in Israel, where I ultimately worked my way up to head trader running the trading room. And then in September of 1984, I met my wife, Joyce, and a few months later we were married. We rented an apartment in the Flatbush section of Brooklyn, and in the summer of 1986, we bought a house in the Bayswater section of Far Rockaway. I had come full circle.

In 1991, there were all kinds of rumors about the bank being sold, so I decided to move on. I went to work trading currencies for a commodities firm. Unfortunately, the bottom fell out of the currency market a year later, forcing the firm to shut down. Joyce and I had just had our third child, and I needed to find a new job right away. This proved to be more difficult than I expected.

After going on several unsuccessful interviews, my brother-in-law said to me, "You know, if you take off your yarmulke, you stand a much better chance of getting hired."

I had always worn my yarmulke and had never taken it off for any reason. So my retort was simple, "If they're not going to hire me because I am an Orthodox Jew who wears a yarmulke, then that is not a place that I want to work." I was not going to deny who I was simply to get a job. It went against my nature. But thankfully, my career path was about to take a major turn.

In 1993, the president of Cantor Fitzgerald was Howard Lutnick, somebody I knew from my earlier tenure at UMB Bank. Howard was the broker who had covered our account. During those years, we had become very close and I would often invite him to our home for the Jewish holidays. At the time, he drove a Porsche 911 Carrera, and invariably he would show up to my house right after Joyce had lit the holiday candles. Once the candles were lit, we weren't allowed to do any work, including driving. I remember she once said to Howard, "Can you please come a little earlier next time? I just want to take the car for a spin around the block."

After having no luck finding a job elsewhere, I decided to call him up and tell him I was looking for a job. It turned out he needed somebody to monitor the firm's expenses. And, because, he told me, I was probably the most honest guy he knew, he offered me the position. It was a moment that made me realize the importance of having a good name. I immediately accepted his offer; and from that day on, I worked for Cantor Fitzgerald, reporting to their offices at the World Trade Center, always wearing my yarmulke.

Working out of offices at the World Trade Center was an amazing experience. My office was on the 101st floor, and each floor was an enormous 50,000 square feet. The view was breathtaking. I looked out over three bridges and was able to see all the way to JFK Airport. I remember a day one summer I called my wife and asked her what she was doing. She said that she was barbecuing. I told her to go inside because it was about to rain. She looked up at the sky and told me there wasn't a cloud in the sky. I insisted that in five minutes she was going to get drenched, and sure enough, five minutes later it started to pour. I was actually able to see the storm heading her way. Another time, on my way into the building, I noticed beautiful white fluffy clouds in the sky. When I got up to my office and looked out the window, the only thing visible was the top of the Empire State Building jutting out from the clouds. The view was completely surreal.

The World Trade Center complex itself was incredible, as well. It was like a city. There was a mall, atrium, stores and eateries. Once you were in the complex, you literally didn't have to leave it for any other reason than to go home.

Working in the World Trade Center gave me a certain feeling that's hard to describe. We were working at the top of the world, and at times it almost felt like having a power over all the other people who worked below.

When I started at Cantor Fitzgerald, I left the trading side of the industry and shifted to the administrative side, where I managed all of the firm's expenses and ran the Business Administration group. Things were going well, Joyce and I had four children by now, and in 1998, we bought a house in Cedarhurst, Long Island. Cedarhurst is a village in an area called the Five Towns, located on the South Shore of Long Island. It was an up-and-coming neighborhood with a lot of young Jewish Orthodox couples with small children moving in. We fit right in. There were many choices of yeshivas to choose from for our children, and there were many synagogues to choose from as well. I had checked out many of them and decided on the one around the corner from my house. Rabbi Spiegel, better known as "The Rebbe," was the spiritual leader. He was a very warm and loving individual, and he made everybody feel at home.

In 2000, the CFO of the firm, Jeff Goldflam, asked me if I would take over global accounts receivables. He was fairly new to the firm, but from the conversations that we had I knew that he was a special person, so I agreed to take the job. He'd soon become a very dear friend of mine, and when he was killed on 9/11, I was devastated.

ARI SCHONBRUN

CHAPTER 2

September 11, 2001, was a Tuesday. It was a magnificent fall day. The sun shone brightly, and the sky was impossibly blue and clear. I remember it was warm outside, with a slight breeze. Just perfect. Had this been a normal day for me, I would've left my house at about 7:30 a.m., allowing me to get to the office at about 8:45 a.m. Yet this Tuesday was exactly a week before Rosh Hashanah, the Jewish New Year. For any religious Jew, the holidays surrounding the New Year—there are a total of five, and most of them last two days—mark a joyful, family-oriented time. They also present one with major work interruptions and scheduling challenges, since work is not permitted on these days. In 2001, all of the holidays ended up falling on Tuesdays, Wednesdays and Thursdays. Between the holidays and the need to leave early on Fridays because of the Sabbath, I knew I'd be missing quite a lot of work. So that September I decided to make it my business to get in extra early and stay extra late—I couldn't afford to fall too far behind with my work.

At about 6:45 a.m. that Tuesday, I had my cup of coffee in one hand, my briefcase in the other, and was ready to go. I yelled upstairs to Joyce and the kids, "Goodbye, I love you!" but right as I was about to slip out the door, Joyce yelled down to me, "Did you do Baruch's book order?"

Baruch, who was eight at the time, is my third child. For anyone not familiar with the book order procedure, let me explain: teachers have a wonderful way of torturing parents. It's called the Scholastic Book Order. In class, the teacher distributes pamphlets that include lists of books and games. The children take them home, and with the help of their parents, they pick out the ones they want to buy. The parents then fill out a tear sheet and enclose a check for the children to bring back to school the next day. About three weeks later, the books and games arrive. The concept is to help the kids get into the habit of reading. It's a wonderful idea; unless, of course, you are working fourteen-hour days and have a two-and-a-half-hour roundtrip commute; then, you really don't have the time for the Scholastic Book Order.

While Joyce was the one who often took care of these kinds of things, Baruch was being very stubborn about the number of books and games that he wanted, so the whole ordering task had been turned over to me. I was supposed to do it with him the previous night, but because of the late hours I'd been keeping, he had already fallen asleep by the time I arrived home.

I was forced to admit to Joyce that I hadn't yet helped Baruch with the book order. She replied rather sternly, "Well then, you're not leaving the house until you do it."

And so I put my coffee and briefcase down, went into the kitchen and proceeded to "negotiate" with my eight year-old for the next twenty minutes. By the time we were done, I had managed to whittle his list down to two book and no games, so I was feeling pretty proud of myself. Interestingly enough, the two books that he chose were from a series called "Survivor." Three weeks later when those books arrived, I got a chill down my spine. It felt like an omen. What was more bizarre was that the book order had actually been overdue. It was supposed to be submitted on Monday, September 10, but Baruch had left the pamphlet at school on Friday, so we couldn't fill it out. On Monday, Joyce sent a note asking the teacher, Mrs. Hefetz, if Baruch could have an extra day extension. Thankfully, the teacher agreed and put the pamphlet into Baruch's knapsack on Monday so that he'd be sure to take it home. Had he brought that pamphlet home as he was supposed to on that Friday, I would've been in my office sometime between 8:00 a.m. and 8:30 a.m. on September 11, 2001—and somebody else would be writing a completely different story.

That morning, with the book order completed, I picked up my briefcase and my now-cold cup of coffee and headed out into what seemed like any ordinary Tuesday.

during

ARI SCHONBRUN

CHAPTER 3

Back then I used to drive from my home in Cedarhurst into Far Rockaway, park my car in the
parking lot of the shopping center on Mott Avenue,
then walk across the street to the elevated platform
to wait for the A train. I took the A train because
it left me off inside the complex of the World Trade
Center. The Mott Avenue stop was the train's first
stop, so I always got a seat. The ride took about an
hour, and then it was only a five-minute walk under-
ground through the mall until I reached One World
Trade Center. That morning I arrived at the building
at approximately 8:40 a.m.

In the main lobby of the building, there were 12 express elevators that went from the lobby straight to the 78th floor. These elevators could hold about 50 people and traveled at a speed of 27 feet per second. They could go from the ground floor to the top in less than a minute. The middle elevator actually went all the way up to the 107th floor, but that was only for people going up to the Windows of the World restaurant.

The 78th floor was designed as a sky lobby. It was where you were let out after taking the lobby elevators to transfer to a "local" elevator to take you to the higher floors. The entire 78th floor was open from one side to the other and had floor-to-ceiling windows that flooded the floor with brilliant natural light. The floor was carpeted in brown with a patchwork design. On one side of the lobby were the large elevators that came up from the lobby, and on the opposite side were the smaller local elevators that went from the 78th floor to all of the higher floors. At the far end of the floor was an escalator that went to the 79th floor. In the middle of the floor, nestled between the two banks of elevators, was a security/information station—usually manned by just one person. Opposite the security station, in between the large elevator banks, was a hallway that led to a security office behind the elevators.

Getting on the elevators at the lobby level had its own procedure. To reach them, you had to go through turnstiles; but in order to get through the turnstiles, you had to swipe through with your ID. The Windows of the World elevator was blocked on either side, and it separated the lobby elevators into two distinct areas, so if you went through the turnstiles on one side of that elevator bank, you couldn't get to the elevators on the other side. Since I was running late that morning, I decided to scope out which elevator was coming first and let that determine which turnstiles to go through. It just so happened that the first elevator to arrive was all the way on the right side of the lobby. I quickly ran over to the turnstiles by that elevator, swiped my ID, went through the turnstile and then got on the elevator. Because I'd chosen this particular elevator, when I got out on the 78th floor, I had to walk all the way back across the sky lobby to the other side since the elevator bank that I needed was all the way on the left side of the building.

I began walking across the sky lobby to the opposite side. I must have been about eight feet away from the elevator I needed to get on when all of a sudden, there was a huge explosion. It felt—and sounded—as if a bomb had exploded in the elevator in front of me. That was my first thought. The entire building shook. The lights went out, and the floor instantly filled with smoke. I am not embarrassed to admit that I screamed as I was thrown off my feet and onto the ground. I could hear people shouting about a fire in the elevator. I was petrified, scared momentarily senseless. It was eerie—like something out of *The Twilight Zone*—to hear the screaming but to not be able to see anyone.

While on the ground, I looked around and saw an emergency light shining between two banks of the large elevators. I decided to head toward that light. I remembered learning as a child that if you are in a place that has smoke you need to stay low to the ground, so I literally crawled on my stomach, like a soldier in battle, toward the light. When I got to the light, I stood up and checked myself out to make sure that I had all of my body parts. After being thrown from the explosion, I was not sure if I had been hurt or not. I thanked God that I seemed to be okay.

I then went behind the elevator banks, where I found the security office. I had worked in that building for eight years and had never known there was an office on that floor. As I opened the door, there was a female security guard sitting on the floor with her back against the wall, crying her eyes out. As unnerving as that was, seeing her crying like that, it gave me a certain level of comfort to know I wasn't alone.

I leaned over to her and said, "Ma'am, calm down. We're going to be okay. Just get a hold of yourself. We are going to be fine." I'm not sure if it was the calm in my voice or my reassurance, but she ultimately calmed down and stopped crying.

As I walked into the office, I saw a guy who identified himself as the fire warden for the floor. He was a short, Hispanic fellow who spoke with an accent. On each floor in the building, there was someone who was designated to be the person the building management would contact in case of an emergency, and who was to then forward the instructions to the rest of the people on that floor.

I approached the fire warden and asked, "What do we do? Where do we go?"

He looked at me, drew a deep breath and said, "I don't know."

That was far from reassuring. After all, if he didn't know, how was I ever going to know? Just then, a woman in a green suit walked through the door. She was covered head-to-toe in soot. I had no idea where she'd come from but it was clear that she was in complete shock. She had a blank stare on her face, almost like a zombie.

I led her into the room and asked if she would like to sit down and she just nodded. I asked if she wanted something to drink, but again, she just nodded. I had never encountered someone in shock. It was scary to witness and I wasn't sure what to do. So I got her a cup of water and sat her down. The fire warden kept trying the phones but he wasn't getting through. The landlines were totally dead.

In the meantime, I looked in the side pouch of my briefcase and realized that a bunch of papers and bills that I was going to mail were missing. I quickly ran back into the hall and sure enough my papers were all in a neat pile on the floor. I guess they fell out when I was thrown to the ground. I scooped them up and quickly headed back to the security office. Just as I entered the office, another security officer suddenly came in; and like the first one, she was crying her eyes out. The one thing I immediately noticed about her was that she had a two-way radio.

I quickly walked over and grabbed her and said, "Ma'am, you have a radio. You can get us help. You need to calm down and get a hold of yourself. You need to get on that radio, and you need to get us help *now*."

She began to collect herself and then, whimpering, she got on the radio and said, "We're on…on…on… the seventy… seventy eighth fl… fl… floor. We… we… nee… nee… need help." But there so much chatter on the radio that no communications were able to get through. We realized, to our dismay, that we weren't going to get any help that way.

I decided to go back out to the hall to see if I couldn't try to find a way out. As I walked into the hall, I encountered a coworker of mine, Virginia DiChiara. It was then, when I saw the condition she was in, that the horribleness of whatever had happened, began to truly sink in.

ARI SCHONBRUN

CHAPTER 4

Virginia and I didn't have an easy history with each other. She was an internal auditor who had been hired a year earlier at Cantor Fitzgerald, and her first task was to audit my department. She came on at the end of the August—my busiest time of the year. I had been the head of the Business Administration department, monitoring all of the firm's expenses. Part of my job was managing the stock of all of Cantor's season tickets for sporting events. The end of August through the beginning of September was the U.S. Open tennis tournament. At the same time, football season was starting, and it was the end of baseball's regular season, with the playoffs set to soon begin. I was putting in 12 to 14 hour days and didn't have a minute to breathe. The last thing that I had time for was an audit. I politely requested that she come back to me in four weeks; at which point, I would be happy to give her whatever she needed. Apparently, however, her boss didn't seem to care about my already-full schedule, because almost immediately I got a call from my boss telling me I was to give Virginia what she needed right away.

Virginia was a tough lady. She would lash into me and my staff to such a degree that she made it seem like she thought we weren't capable of doing anything right. That was bad enough, but then the situation escalated. She began writing us up for all kinds of things, which cast us all in the worst possible light. I felt like I was under attack. And in fact, it reached the point where she almost got me fired. It was the worst time of my career.

By the time Virginia had completed her audit, it was decided that my department needed to be disbanded and that all of my staff would be dispersed throughout other parts of the company. I myself was transferred to the accounting department, where I was put in charge of global accounts receivables, reporting directly to Jeff Goldflam, the CFO. Jeff was a wonderful man. He, more than anyone, gave me my self-esteem back, during a time when I was feeling really low. Not only was he a terrific boss, but he also was a great human being. He once gave one piece of advice that has stuck with me to this day. He told me if I wanted to be successful that I should, "Speak British, Think Yiddish." I miss him greatly.

Now as for Virginia and me, on September 11, 2001, it seemed our paths were destined to cross again, in a way that would forever alter our relationship. As she tells it, on that morning, like me, she was also making her way to work slightly later than usual. She was normally out of the house and on her way to work by 7 a.m. But that morning was so brilliantly beautiful she decided to dillydally. She let her two golden retrievers play in the yard, cooked herself some eggs, and poured herself a cup of coffee. "I was just moseying along," she says, "I didn't feel like rushing." She left her Bloomfield,

New Jersey, home at 7:40 a.m.; this forty-minute delay would end up saving her life. It was just after 8:40 a.m. when she entered the lobby of the North Tower of the World Trade Center. Together with a Cantor Fitzgerald coworker, she rode the elevator up to the 78th floor, where she crossed the lobby in order to take a second elevator the rest of the way to her office on the 101st floor.

The elevator door open and she pressed the button for 101. It was 8:46 a.m. As the elevator doors closed, Flight 11 crashed into the northern face of Tower One about fourteen floors above. The elevator went black and "bounced around like a ball," Virginia recalls.

"I remember seeing two lines shooting around the top of the elevator," electrical cables that had come loose and were spitting current, "and everybody started screaming."

In front of Virginia was a man named Roy Bell, who later said that the sound of the impact was "deafening, like someone banging a two-by-two sheet of aluminum with a hammer, six inches from your head." The right wall of the elevator car crashed into Bell, breaking several of his fingers and flinging him to the left side. Miraculously, the elevator doors remained open about a foot. Within seconds, the jet fuel that had been coming down the sides of the elevator was ignited by the sparking cables and Bell "just sprinted" out of the elevator. Virginia had been crouching down behind Bell, and when she saw Bell go through, she thought, "I don't hear any screaming, so I know he's not on fire... I'm outta here." She decided to go for it, but as she gathered herself, huge blue flames—translucent teardrops of fire, a foot in diameter—began cascading down in a steady curtain. Virginia dropped her bag, her elbows pushing the black rubber guards on the elevator doors. Left behind was a Cantor coworker. Virginia never saw her again, a fact that would haunt her for a long time.

When she emerged from the elevator, Virginia was on fire.

"I remember hearing my hair on fire," she says.

(She later joked, "I must have put on some extra hair spray.")

With her hands, she patted out the flames. "I got it out, I got it out," she said to herself. Then, feeling something else entirely different and hot, she looked back and saw flames rising from her shoulder. In that instant, she remembered the old lesson from grade school: stop, drop and roll. She threw herself to the carpeted floor and rolled over and over, frantically patting out the flames.

"I remember getting up and just looking at myself," she says, then continuing with her memory, recalls thinking at the time. "Okay, everything's out. But then I sort of started laughing, almost like hysteria, like a giggle, thinking, 'Oh my God, let me do it again just in case I missed it.' I was so scared, like there was an ember on my body that was still going to flare up."

Virginia crawled some twenty feet down the hallway and sat with her back propped against a wall. She was wearing a sleeveless cotton shirt that day, and her arms and hands were seared with third-degree burns. In shock, she did not feel the pain—yet. Improbably prosaic thoughts crossed her mind. In the briefcase she'd left on the elevator were some airplane tickets recently purchased for a vacation to the Florida Keys, as well as a wad of cash. Should she go back and retrieve it? "No," she thought to herself. "Just stay right where you are." Then she spotted me.

"Ari!" she called out. I turned around and looked at her. "Virginia! Oh my God!"

ARI SCHONBRUN

CHAPTER 5

I rushed over to where Virginia stood. She started walking toward me. "Ari, thank God. Please help me. I am in so much pain. Please help me and whatever you do, please don't leave me."

At that point, whatever our history was no longer mattered. I looked at her and the only thing that went through my mind was, here is another human being who is in terrible shape; she needs my help, and I was the one that God had chosen to be there for her.

I looked at her and said, "Virginia, I promise I will help you, and I promise I won't leave you. We will get out of here."

I then led her into the security office and sat her down. I poured a cup of water for her, but she couldn't hold the cup. How heavy is an eight ounce plastic cup of water? And yet she couldn't hold it. That's how bad her hands were burned. I had to pour the water into her mouth so she could drink. Roy Bell had also made it to the security office. His doctors would later tell him that the few seconds between his exit and Virginia's made the difference between his second-degree and her third-degree burns.

I turned to the fire warden. "Anything yet?"

"No, nothing."

I went back outside, looking for a way out. I had no idea where to go. I went back inside. All of a sudden, the fire warden turned to me and said, "Okay, we can get out. Stairwell on the left."

I will never forget those words, "stairwell on the left."

When I was in my office on the 101st floor and needed to go to other Cantor floors, I would always take the stairs. It was much quicker than waiting for the elevators. I knew where the staircases were on those floors, but here on the 78th, I had no idea where the stairs were located.

We walked out of the office, and it was then that I noticed a sign that, to this very day, I look for whenever I enter any building. It is usually red and white. It reads "Exit." It sounds funny but that sign helped save our lives that day. We walked toward that sign and somebody had suddenly run ahead of us. He went around the bend and sure enough there was a door there. He opened it, and yelled out, "I found it!"

I looked at Virginia. She seemed to be panic-stricken and trembling. "Virginia, we are getting out of here."

It was 9 a.m. as we made our way to the stairway on the 78th floor of the burning North Tower. Virginia says that all she could think about was how hard it was to put one foot in front of the other. She did stop to take one last look in the direction of the elevator she had escaped from; it was no longer there. "It was a black hole," she says, recalling what she then saw.

We walked toward the door, and I noticed that there were lights on in the stairwell. There were about eight or ten of us altogether, and I'm not sure what possessed me, but I turned to the group and asked, "Does anybody have a flashlight?" I knew that if the lights were to go out, it would be pitch black.

Two people actually answered and said, "I have a flashlight."

I remember my first thought was "where did you get a flashlight from and why are you carrying it?" But the answer didn't matter. I turned to the group and said, "Listen people, if the lights in the stairwell go out nobody should panic. We have flashlights, so we will have light."

The next thing I did was look down at Virginia's feet, and I said to myself, "Thank God, she's wearing flats." It sounds funny now, but there were high heels scattered throughout the stairwell, all the way down. Women had kicked them off to be able to run down as fast as they could.

Once we reached the stairwell, Virginia turned to me and asked, "How the hell am I going to do it?"

"You're going to make it," I said, reassuring her.

Virginia held her arms out, Frankenstein-like, careful not to let anyone or anything touch them. Then we started to head down the stairs. It was the fire warden first, then Roy Bell, then me, with Virginia right behind me. I actually didn't recall the order until I met with Virginia several months later, and she reminded me that I told her, "If you feel faint, Virginia, fall forward, fall on me."

Roy Bell was not happy about that prospect because what if I was unable to support her weight. Then it would be both me and Virginia on top of Roy! Thank God we didn't have to live that scenario.

When we got down to the 75th floor, what felt to me like one of the biggest miracles of that entire day occurred; besides, of course, that I wasn't killed when the plane hit. My cell phone rang. Today, that doesn't sound like such a big deal, but back then there weren't as many cell phone towers. Cell phone service in the Trade Center was almost always non-existent, and it was even worse on the higher floors. I remember standing in my office many times right up against my window, and I'd still not get a signal. Now, here I was standing in the middle of the building, in a stairwell on a day when there was no signal available at all, and somehow my phone rang. I was shocked. I answered the phone. "Hello??"

It was my wife on the other end of that phone. She was crying and telling me something about a plane going into the building. I had no idea what she was talking about. She kept talking and crying and finally I stopped her and said, "Joyce, I am in a stairwell. I am on the 75th floor. I am on my way down. *Now is not a good time*. I will call you when I get out of the building," and I hung up. At that point, Roy Bell realized I had service on my phone.

"Oh my God, Ari, can I use your phone to call my wife?" Roy asked.

"Of course you can you use my phone," I said, as I handed it to him.

Roy dialed his wife, hit send and… nothing. The signal was now dead. I then realized what an amazing miracle had just occurred. I looked up toward the heavens and said, "Thank You." At least my wife knew that I was alive, and as strange it may seem, given what was going on, that gave me great comfort.

We continued making our way down, reaching about the 50th floor, when Virginia turned to me and said, "Ari, I can't go on."

My first thought was to let her sit down, gather some strength and then continue on. But I immediately thought to myself that if she sat down she may never get up, and if she doesn't get up, there'd be a greater chance that we would die—and dying was not on my agenda that day. I looked her square in the eye and said, "Virginia, you can do this. We need to keep moving."

Somebody had a bottle of Poland Spring water. I don't remember who it was or where it came from, but I do remember that the firefighters were breaking open vending machines so people could get drinks because of the increasing heat in the building. I took the bottle of water and poured it into Virginia's mouth, and then I poured it on her arms to try and give her some relief from the pain. Around this time, I became a coach and started giving her encouragement. I also began counting down the floors as we progressed, "45, 44, 43, 42... You're doing great, let's keep moving." And move we did, all the way to 38. When we reached the 38th floor, it was packed with people. As we approached them, I remember one woman turned around to see who was coming, and when she saw Virginia, she shouted, "Ugh!"

Virginia turned and said, "Ari, how bad is it?"

"You look great, Virginia. Don't worry about it.

You're going to be fine," I responded, knowing I had to continue to reassure her. I know that I lied about how great she looked. And I wasn't actually sure if I was lying about her condition. I honestly didn't know if she was going to be all right. The only thing I did know was that I needed to keep her spirits up and that we needed to keep moving or else we'd all be in serious trouble.

"Is there a paramedic in the building?" I started to shout out. "If you are a paramedic, please help us. We have a burn victim here and need help. If you are a paramedic, please come and help. Otherwise please step to the right and let us through so that we can get help." The next thing we knew, the people just moved. They all squeezed as far as they possibly could to the right, creating an aisle that allowed us to get through. It was like the splitting of the Red Sea when the Israelites left Egypt: I couldn't believe it. The stairwell was only two-people-wide, but all these people made enough space so that we could get down before them.

I soon realized that the reason people were stuck on the 38th floor was because they needed to make room to let the firefighters up. I remember stopping on a landing at about the 36th floor to let a couple of firefighters go by. I can still remember the faces of two of them: one had glasses, the other a moustache. They were carrying at least 50 pounds of gear, and I remember thinking how brave these guys were and that you couldn't pay me enough to do their job. I don't know if they made it out, but I had nightmares about them for many months afterwards. I always had a feeling that they never made it out.

ARI SCHONBRUN

CHAPTER 6

We continued making our way down at a decent pace considering Virginia's condition. By now it was just the four of us: Virginia, Roy Bell, the fire warden (I never did find out his name) and me. The firefighters had held everyone else up that were originally with us from the 78th floor. When we got down to the 8th floor, there was water all over the place. It was up to our ankles.

I turned to Virginia and said, "Virginia, real slow. Please, take it real slow." I knew that if she were to slip in the water and fall, there'd be no way for me to pick her up. Her burns were so severe that you couldn't even touch her, let alone hold her.

I was wearing a brand new pair of pants that day, and when I saw all of the water, I got nervous that I might ruin my pants, and that my wife would be livid. God, the stupid things that were going through my mind. But I was so nervous about my pants that I lifted them up so they wouldn't get wet and proceeded to walk down. After about a flight, I realized that holding them up was futile, so I just let them down. I figured I'd suffer the consequences later when (if) I got home.

When we reached the first floor, the fire warden, who'd been leading the whole way, kept going down.

"Where are we going?" I asked him.

"We have to go out through the garage."

I turned to Virginia. "We have to get out through the garage. That's about another four or five flights. No big deal, we just came down seventy-eight flights, what's another four or five?"

We went down about two flights when all of a sudden the door opened on the first floor and a voice yelled down, "Where are you people going?"

"We're going out through the garage," I yelled back up.

"You can't get out through the garage! You have to come back up here and come out through the first floor."

I turned to Virginia and said, "We have to go back up two flights."

She said a few choice words, which I would not use in mixed company, or any company for that matter; and we then proceeded to walk back up. Later on, I heard that there were people in the garage who never made it out.

Who was the guy who opened the door? I have no idea. I never saw anybody. I just heard a voice. Why did he pick that exact moment to open the door? I don't know. The fact that he did was one more twist of fate that were adding up as each hour of this day passed. Maybe it was a person; maybe it was an angel. I have no idea. All I know is that if he hadn't been there at that moment, there is a very good chance that we wouldn't have survived. Somebody (God?) was looking out for us that fateful day.

When we finally got out of the stairwell, it took me a moment to recognize where we were. At first, it didn't look familiar, but then I saw the sign "Coffee Station" and I immediately realized that it was the coffee station right before the lobby of Tower One. Many a morning I had bought my coffee there on my way up to the office. Once I had my bearings, I knew that the fastest way out of the building would be to go through the revolving doors into the lobby of Tower One, head across the lobby to the other side and then through the revolving doors that would lead us out of the building.

I was just about to begin leading the way when a police officer and firefighter came up to us and escorted us out the other way. They made us walk through the concourse, past all of the stores, toward the WB store at the very end of the concourse, then left to the escalators (which weren't working), then up and out onto Church Street.

It wasn't until later that I found out why they took us that way when clearly the way I originally planned to go would've been a much quicker way out. Had we gone my way, it would have led us out onto West Street—and that was where the people were jumping or falling from the towers onto the ground. I thank God every day that we went the other way. When I later saw that scene on TV, I was horrified. Had I actually been there to witness it, I don't know how I possibly could have survived the sight and remained sane.

As we were walking through the concourse, Virginia turned to me and said, "Ari, please call my mom. Tell her I'm okay. Also, tell her to call my cousin and let her know that I'm okay."

"Give me the number, and I promise I will Virginia, but can we get out of the building first?"

With that, she gave me the number and I put it in my phone.

ARI SCHONBRUN

CHAPTER 7

When we reached the top of the broken escalators, we saw the doors that led out of the building. There were police and firefighters urging everybody to go uptown. As we looked outside, we saw people running in that direction.

I approached one of the cops, "I have a burn victim here. Where should we go?"

"Burn victim? Go across the street in front of the Millennium Hotel. They are setting up a triage center, and there will be ambulances there very soon."

I took Virginia across the street, but no ambulances had yet arrived. Somebody in charge told Virginia to sit on the curb. Virginia looked down and saw a woman sitting on the curb, who was bleeding from her head and face.

"I'm not sitting down there," she said to me.

"Okay, no problem. Just lean on me," I said to her. I remember the following day in one of the newspapers there was a picture of that same woman who'd been sitting on the curb, bleeding.

An ambulance came along soon after and I helped Virginia get inside. I remember breathing a sigh of relief. I knew she wasn't in good shape, but at least now she was getting medical attention. I stepped out of the ambulance, turned around and looked up. This was the first time that I saw the buildings on fire. I knew that a plane had gone into Tower One, which was why it was on fire, but I had no idea what had happened to Tower Two. I just assumed that the wind had blown the fire over to Tower Two. I hadn't heard anything while in the stairwell on the way down, and *I had never heard the second plane hit.*

"How did Tower Two get on fire?" I asked a guy standing next to me.

"Are you kidding? Two jetliners went into the

buildings. They're calling it a terrorist attack."

I looked at him like he was crazy. "What are you talking about?" I asked, and suddenly got really scared.

I took out my cell phone and began trying to call people, but I couldn't get through to anyone. For the next several minutes, I kept pacing around near the ambulance, trying to see if I could get a signal. I turned around to one of the paramedics, "Excuse me, do you know why I can't get signal on my phone?"

"You won't be able to get a signal around here. There's too much equipment."

I thought to myself, this guy has no idea what he's talking about. So I kept walking around, trying to get a signal, though never strolling too far away from the ambulance. Every few minutes, I'd go into the ambulance to check on Virginia to see how she was doing. The paramedics were tending to her and two other victims, giving her water, clipping her shirt and bra off and draping a gown over her. She was sitting up as they worked on her. They kept trying to put an IV needle into her hand, but it just wouldn't stay in. The first layer of skin was gone, so there was nothing to hold the needle in place. He tried taping it but it didn't hold. Virginia was in agony. Later she'd tell me, "It was like someone was tearing the skin off of me. It was excruciating."

"I'm going to pass out," she said to me, as she sat upright in the ambulance. She rocked herself back and forth, but she didn't pass out.

"Why aren't we leaving? Why can't I lie down?" she asked the paramedic.

"We're expecting a huge amount of casualties and we need room for as many people as possible. We can't leave until we fill the ambulance, and we have the capacity to take seven or eight people."

Virginia couldn't find a position to make her even slightly more comfortable. I also didn't know what to do with myself, where to put myself or where to go. I stepped out of the ambulance once again. I was beside myself, and I was at an absolute loss about what to do. I couldn't call anybody. As much as I wanted to look for more of my friends and coworkers I couldn't go back into the building because I couldn't possibly leave Virginia. So I kept asking the ambulance driver, "When are you leaving?" He must've thought I was such a nudge.

Finally, the ambulance driver said, "Okay, we're ready to go."

I immediately thought, "Great, they'll take Virginia to the hospital, she'll get medical attention, and then I can head back to the building to look for more friends and coworkers."

All of a sudden Virginia turned to me and said, "Ari, you're coming with us."

It was a very awkward moment. I can't possibly say that I was in a comfort zone with all that was going on, but the reality is that it was familiar territory. I knew where I was, and I knew that if I had to get out of there, I would be able figure out where to go. I honestly didn't want to leave the area.

"Virginia," I said, "you don't need me anymore. The ambulance is going to take to you to the hospital, and I will get in touch with your mom and she will meet you at the hospital. You are going to be fine."

She turned to the ambulance driver and pointed at me. *"We're not leaving unless 'he' comes with us."*

I remember seeing the look in the driver's eyes. He must've been thinking to himself, "this isn't a taxi."

He looked at me, and I looked at him. Finally I said

to him, "Maybe I should go? It would probably be a good thing for her psychologically, if I go with her."

"Okay," he said to me. "Hop in the front."

I climbed into the front of the ambulance and we pulled out. At the time, I had no idea, but this was how I was driven away from my own, otherwise certain, death. It turned out that we were one of only a few ambulances that survived the collapse of the towers. I have many friends who belong to a volunteer ambulance corps called Hatzalah, and several days later they showed me pictures of many ambulances that had been crushed under falling concrete and debris.

Virginia thanks me every day for saving her life. But I always tell her, "Virginia, you got it all wrong. Who saved whose life? If you hadn't insisted that I get in that ambulance, I'd be dead. I would have been standing at that base of that building when it came down."

Who saved whose life? Had I not met her in the hallway, would I have been able to get down and out of the building as fast as we did? For all I know, I could still have been in the building when it came down. Who saved whose life?

CHAPTER 8

As the ambulance drove away from the chaos and destruction toward St. Vincent's Hospital on Seventh Avenue at Twelfth Street, I remember the driver saying that we would take the streets, not the highway. The streets were absolutely filled with people. Everybody was holding a camera of some sort: video cameras, still cameras, digital cameras. Yet the one thing everyone had in common was a look of utter disbelief. Mouths agape, everyone looked to be in shock.

I remember when we finally reached St. Vincent's and pulled up to the emergency room, all of the doctors and nurses were standing outside, waiting. Lined up next to them were rows of gurneys and wheel-chairs. These folks were ready. They were waiting for a steady, unending stream of casualties and injured to be rushed to the hospital. Unfortunately, most of those gurneys and wheelchairs would remain empty and unused—hardly any victims came to the hospi-tals. Either you escaped the buildings that day and were okay, or you were in the towers or near them, and when they came down, you were killed.

They put Virginia in a wheelchair and took her into the hospital. To this day, I have no idea why they didn't put her on a gurney. It has always both-ered me. They immediately started to ask her for her personal information. I knew all of it after hear-ing her answer these same questions several times when we had initially gotten into the ambulance, so I was answering for her. They wheeled her into the emergency room and to my surprise, they let me go right in with her. And it was good thing they had, because they put her in a corner, closed the curtain, and quickly left. She was in agony and couldn't find a comfortable position. With her arms killing her, she had nowhere to rest them.

I pulled over a large garbage can and told her to rest them on it. She looked at me like I was crazy, "I'm not resting my arms on a garbage can." I realized that there was nothing that I could do for her and decided to try and get help. I walked outside the curtain, and shouted, "Hello, is anybody here? I have a burn victim here and she needs help!"

A nurse came over, "What's the problem?"

"Look behind the curtain and you'll see what the problem is," I said to her.

She looked at the Virginia and said, "I'll be right back with a doctor."

She returned with a doctor, but by now, I was agitated. "Can you help her please? She is writhing in pain."

"Who are you?" the doctor asked. "Are you a relative?"

"No, I'm her coworker. I helped to bring her here."

"You're going to have to leave," he said to me.

I was overcome with anger, but there wasn't much I could do. "Virginia, I have to leave. They're not letting me stay. But don't worry, I'll get a hold of your mom and she'll be here soon."

With those final words, I started to leave the hospital. Walking out, I passed a long room that had a line of desks and phones. I figured, what the heck? So I walked in and went toward a desk to use a phone, but a nurse spotted me.

"Who are you and what are you doing in here?"

"I came in because I needed to use your phone."

"Get out of here. You can't be in here," she demanded.

Did they not know that there was an emergency the likes of which the city—the country—had never before experienced? Why the hospital couldn't show common courtesy still makes no sense to me. Thinking back at how we were treated, I realize just how strange the staff's reaction was. There we were at St. Vincent's, within sight of the World Trade Center, with an unfathomably horrific emergency in progress, and the staff, even though they were trained as emergency personnel, didn't seem to acknowledge that Virginia and I were survivors of it. Instead, these people were acting with bureaucratic mindsets of "old rules." It was as if we weren't even there. Our lack of treatment and attention is in retrospect even more bizarre, if not disturbing, because St. Vincent's became the city's primary admitting hospital for those injured on 9/11. Virginia must have been one of the first patients admitted that day. I can only imagine that the staff was, at that precise moment, in a state of shock. Yet, still to this day, the way they treated us baffles me.

I walked out onto the street and tried to figure out what to do. I stood there, completely disoriented. For a moment, I had no idea where I was or how to get anywhere. I tried my phone again, but again I couldn't get through to anyone, so I decided to look for a pay phone. That was an odd feeling. Even by that point in 2001, pay phones had become practically extinct. Who used pay phones? No one, I knew. Everybody had their cell phones, but now they were worthless.

I saw somebody in the street and approached him, "Excuse me, can you tell me where I can find a pay phone?"

"Sorry, I can't help you."

All of a sudden, I heard two people talking behind me. In a voice of disbelief one said to the other, "Wow, did you hear? Tower Two collapsed."

I turned around and from where I was standing,

right outside St. Vincent's Hospital on Seventh Avenue, I had a clear view of the Twin Towers. And sure enough, Tower Two was now gone. I couldn't believe it. The towers were huge, massive buildings. I simply couldn't fathom how they could possibly collapse. Until that moment, I had been alarmed, but all my thoughts had been within the context of a normal, working reality. When I saw the buildings on fire for the first time, after I got Virginia into the ambulance, I remember thinking that this was a pretty bad fire. You certainly couldn't help but notice the huge gaping hole in Tower One. But when the firefighters passed us on their way up I figured that they would get the fire under control. I assumed maybe it would take a month or two to get the building back in shape. Heck, I had thought to myself, I could use a vacation. But a total collapse. No way.

Yet there I was standing looking and there it was—or wasn't. This was no longer something I could rationally comprehend. This was total, cataclysmic disaster. To say that it was disaster of "biblical proportions" seemed apt. It was most definitely a disaster I had never imagined I would see with my own eyes. With every passing second, I felt more and more scared. I didn't know where I was, had no way to get in touch with anyone, and had absolutely no idea where to go. All of a sudden, I saw a guy walking down the street, speaking into his cell phone. And like so many times that day, the most mundane, if not idiotic thought flashed through my mind: when this is all over, I'm going to find out who his carrier is, and I'm going to switch to that one.

I ran over to the guy. "Excuse me, can I use your phone? I have a real emergency." He looked at me and said, "Sure."

"Hey listen," he said into the phone, "some guy needs my phone. I'll call you back."

"Here you go," he said, handing me his phone.

I thanked him and took the phone and started to dial. The first person I called was...Virginia's mom. I told this to my wife six months later. She was sooooo mad. "Why didn't you call me first?" she rightly asked. Yet, all I could tell her was the truth, "I promised Virginia that I would call her mom."

ARI SCHONBRUN

CHAPTER 9

Six months after 9/11, Virginia told me that this was the second time that her parents had lived through something like this. Forty years earlier, Virginia had lost her only brother in a fire. He'd been playing with candles and matches behind the couch in the living room while Virginia watched television and Connie, her mother, prepared breakfast downstairs in the kitchen. Virginia, who was five years old, emerged unscathed. Her brother, though, was charred over 85 percent of his body before his father, Sal, was able to rescue him. He died two weeks later. Connie was sitting by the phone on that bright September morning when she relived her first nightmare, "you never think it's going to happen a second time."

It was 10:30 a.m. when I was finally able to get through to them.

"Hello, Mrs. DiChiara? My name is Ari Schonbrun. I'm a coworker of your daughter, Virginia. She's alive but she has severe burns. She's at St. Vincent's Hospital, and I'd recommend that you get down there right away."

Connie immediately broke down and began to cry, handing the phone to Sal, "Hello?"

I then repeated the information to Sal, and then remembered to tell him that Virginia asked that they call her cousin. I didn't remember her cousin's name, but Sal must've known, because he said okay, and then thanked me for calling and hung up the phone.

I turned to the guy whose phone I was using and asked, "Do you mind if I make one more call?"

He obviously had heard my conversation and now knew where I'd been and said, "Of course."

I dialed my wife's number, hit send, but the call wouldn't go through. The signal was now dead. And I remember thinking to myself, "Guess, I'll forget about that carrier after all."

I handed the man back his phone and asked him if he knew where there was a pay phone. Unsurprisingly, he said he did not, and went on his way. I was now standing in the middle of the street, still without any idea what to do. I looked around me, and all of a sudden I noticed that there was a restaurant across the street at the corner. I said to myself, "Restaurant, they must have a phone."

I ran inside and bumped into a waiter.

"Excuse me, can I use your phone?" I asked.

He looked at me and said, "Well, I don't know. It's not my restaurant. It's not my phone."

I saw in the back of the restaurant that there were two people talking on phones. I left the waiter and went straight to the back where a woman was standing.

She looked at me and asked, "Do you need a phone?"

"Yes, I do."

"You're going to have to wait."

"Wait? I can't wait. This is an emergency."

It was then that I noticed two guys sitting in the restaurant, eating breakfast or lunch. I really didn't know which because I had no idea what time it was; in fact, the first time that I looked at my watch that day was at a quarter to one, but I'll get to that later.

One of the guys turned to me and asked, "Do you need a phone? My apartment is five doors down. You can come to my apartment and use my phone."

Now, this being New York City, I momentarily thought to myself, "Ax murderer?" But I was in such a desperate state that I answered, "Oh yes, thank you so much."

He turned to his friend and said, "I'm gonna go back to my apartment and let this guy use my phone."

He got up, left his buddy and his meal, and started to walk out. I followed right behind him.

We went around the corner and I glanced down the street, past his apartment, and saw a pay phone with a long line of people waiting to use it. A woman, who'd been standing on line waiting, started heading toward us. As she approached, the guy from the restaurant who had offered to help me stopped her and asked if she wanted to use the phone in his apartment.

I could see the look her in eyes, especially since there were two of us, and she must've had the same

"Ax murderer?" thought that I'd had, because she said, "Uh, no thank you," and continued walking.

Once we got to the man's apartment, he opened the door downstairs, turned to the people waiting on line for the pay phone, and said, "If anybody needs a phone, you can come up to my apartment and use mine."

I remember thinking to myself, "Who is this guy and where did come from?" Well, his name was John Roccosalva, and I'll never forget him.

John's apartment building was a walk-up, and I remember thinking, "Oh my God, how many flights up do we have to go?" Fortunately, he lived just one flight up.

He opened the door and pointed to the phone, which was right by the front door. To say the apartment was small is being extravagant. It was a single room with barely enough space for a twin bed, a table with three chairs, a tiny stove and a dorm-sized refrigerator. The walls were white and virtually bare except for a few shelves of books. No television. No radio or stereo. This place was so small you couldn't change your mind in it.

I walked to the phone and started to dial my wife's office. I got a fast busy signal. I tried again, but, again, it was fast busy. I realized there must have been trouble with the lines.

A guy standing behind me asked, "Do you mind if I try?"

I grunted, "Sure go ahead."

He dialed, "Yeah, honey, it's me. I'm in some guy's apartment."

He then quickly hung up and a woman behind him grabbed the receiver and started dialing, "Honey, yeah it's me. I'm fine."

I remember thinking to myself, *"Give me that phone!"*

But I still had presence of mind and manners, so I asked, "Excuse me, do you mind if I try again?"

I took the receiver, dialed, but once again, to my now enormous frustration, got another fast busy signal. I dialed one more time and it started to ring, thank God.

"B'nos Bais Ya'akov, may I help you?"

"Joyce Schonbrun, please."

"Who's calling?

"Her husband!!!"

"Just a moment please."

"No, no wait…" And then I heard the music. She'd put me on hold. I was going nuts. Like many offices, when they put you on hold, you could often end up on "perma-hold." I worried that I'd end up being placed on hold and forgotten about. The wait couldn't have been more than a minute, but it seemed like hours.

"Ari?"

"Yeah, it's me."

Joyce started to cry.

"Honey, what's the matter?"

"Tower One collapsed and I thought you were dead."

The last time she had spoken to me I was on the 75th floor of Tower One. When it collapsed and she hadn't heard from me again, she was convinced that I was now dead and had been trying to figure out how she was going to tell our children that Daddy had been killed. The oldest of my boys was only eight. Since a Jewish boy has to be thirteen to say the *Kaddish* (the mourner's prayer) for a parent, Joyce had been wondering who was going to say the *Kaddish* for me. That day she lived through this nightmare twice: first when the plane hit, and then again, when the building collapsed.

Later, Joyce told me that she had planned on leaving work to go home after the plane hit. But the dean of the school, where she worked as the Director of the Wasserman Learning Center, insisted that she stay since they had six phone lines and, therefore, I had a better chance of reaching her there. She told him, "You don't understand. I need to get to a TV and see what's going on."

He looked her and said, "Wait right here."

At that point, my wife said the greatest miracle of her day happened. The dean returned with a television. This may not seem like a real miracle, but considering that this was a very religious girls school, the norm was that none of the children had televisions in their homes. So she assumed that the school must also have forbidden television, but the dean kept one for videos and presentations.

After we both calmed down, she asked me, "Where are you?"

"I'm in some guy's apartment. His name is John Roccosalva."

"What are you going to do? They shut down the city. They've shut down the bridges, the tunnels, nothing is going in or out. They shut down all public transportation. What are you going to do?"

"I don't know. Maybe I'll go up to Ellie's office."

Ellie was my brother who worked up on Forty-seventh Street and Sixth Avenue.

"Okay, but call me when you get there."

"I will. I love you."

"I love you, too." And then we hung up.

All of a sudden the events of the day started to sink in. The place that I had worked for the past eight and a half years was gone. I was thinking to myself, "How is this possible?" I had this huge pit in my stomach. I was literally about to cry. I felt so all alone. I kept thinking: What happened to my friends, my coworkers? Did they get out? What am I supposed to do now?

I turned to John and said, "John, do you mind if I hang out here a little bit? I need to rest."

I started to take off my shoes and socks, and John

noticed that my socks were wet. "Ohhh, would you like a clean pair of socks? You can have one of mine."

Who was this guy? Was he from Kansas? Actually, he was from Cleveland, but had been living in New York for the better part of thirty years.

"No, thanks John. I'm good."

Perhaps what John did wouldn't have been such a big deal in a small Kansas town, but in New York City, it was extraordinary. He must've invited at least several dozen, maybe even up to a hundred people, who otherwise would not have had any way to contact loved ones to reassure them that they were safe. Long lines snaked around the corner, past the few available pay phones. And John kept going downstairs, asking more and more people if they wanted to come inside to his apartment, which was almost exactly two miles directly north of what would soon become known as Ground Zero.

John later said that opening his apartment to the masses that day was actually therapeutic for him. Early in the morning, he had seen the first plane "sticking out of the North Tower," as he put it; and at first, he and his friend speculated that maybe it was a scene being filmed for a movie. John was unemployed, having been recently laid off from his job arranging window displays. And since he didn't know what to do with himself that day, having people use his phone gave him a project. It allowed him not to think deeply about what had just happened. He was grateful to give people help, if for no other reason than their presence and company allowed him to not feel so otherwise alone.

Today, John works as a florist. He still has no television or radio, but he does pay a bit more attention to world events. He insists he doesn't feel a need to visit Ground Zero. He says he doesn't need a reminder of something he knows he will never forget.

In his apartment that day there was another guy, Martin Walk, who told me that he was a reporter and started to ask me all kinds of questions. I really wasn't in the mood to talk, so I gave him a few brief answers, and then told him that I really didn't feel like answering more questions about what had happened. Five years later, he reached out to me because he wanted to do a story for the fifth year anniversary. I agreed to do it and invited him up to my office. It was during that interview that he told me that John's phone bill for that day was over $300. I felt terrible. If I had known, I would've paid for it, as I'm sure every other person who'd also used his phone would have too.

After having sat in John's apartment for a few minutes, I began to get antsy.

I said to John, "John, I gotta get going."

"Not a problem. Good luck," he replied.

"Thanks," I said. I put my wet shoes and socks back on and headed back out into the street.

CHAPTER 10

When I got outside, I had no idea where I was, but I knew that I needed to get uptown. So I stopped somebody who was walking by and asked, "Excuse me, can you tell me how to get uptown?"

"Uptown? Follow the crowd."

It was then that I noticed everyone was walking in the same direction. So, I followed the crowd. I walked to the corner and realized that I was on Eighth Avenue and Twelfth Street. I then remembered that my good friend Richard Kendall had an office on Ninth Avenue and Fifteenth Street, so I began to walk there.

Richard was in the financial printing business, and his firm had done the printing for Cantor when we took eSpeed public. Another coincidence? I had been the person in charge of sourcing the financial printer, so I was quite familiar with his office, which was incredible, with almost every amenity you could imagine. There was a billiard room, a workout room and beautiful bathrooms. And the bathrooms had showers, but since I didn't have a change of clothes—though I obviously could've used a shower—I didn't think it was worth it.

I walked through the double glass doors and into Richard's office. The receptionist took a look at me and said, "Ari, are you okay?"

I had no idea what I looked like. John didn't have a mirror in his apartment, and the last time I had seen myself was early in the morning before I left home.

"Yeah, I'm fine. Is Richard around?"

"No, he's in Florida. Can I get you anything?"

"Yeah. A conference room, a phone and some water would be great."

She called somebody out to take me to a conference room, where a phone and water waited for me.

I picked up the phone and began to call everybody I knew. Although my cell phone was not working I was able to access the phone book and so I had all the phone numbers that I needed. I called my sister, my sister-in-law, my brother-in-law and my brother. I called a few friends. The only people I couldn't reach that day were my parents. They lived in Israel, and it was impossible to get an international connection. Fortunately my niece, Avivit, who was living in Belgium then, had been able to place an international call from there to the United States. She managed to get through to my sister-in-law, Renee, in West Hempstead, who reassured Avivit that I was alive and well. Avivit was the one who relayed the news to my parents in Israel. It was an enormous relief knowing they already knew I was alive.

At some point a little while later, a guy entered the conference room and asked if I would like some lunch.

"Lunch? What time is it?" I asked.

"A quarter to one." That was the first time I remember looking at my watch that day.

"Thanks, but I am strictly kosher so I don't think you can help me."

"That's not a problem. We have several kosher clients. There's a kosher restaurant across town that we always order from."

"They aren't going to deliver."

"Oh, sure they will. They deliver all the time."

It was obvious that this guy was totally clueless. There was no traffic moving anywhere along the streets. But I figured, what the heck.

"Pastrami on club bread, fries and a Coke."

"No problem. I'll be right back."

A few minutes later, he returned. "They're not going to deliver." He said, then immediately added, "but if you like, we have a pantry and have all kinds of snacks in there. Help yourself."

I thanked him and went to the pantry. I grabbed a few granola bars and chips and an orange juice, and then went back to the conference room to eat my "lunch". Suddenly, somebody came into the room and said that the Empire State Building had just been evacuated. I jumped out of my chair and ran into the main office. They had a TV in there, and I wanted to get the latest updates on what was going on. The problem was, there were so many rumors flying around that day that nobody knew what to believe.

Once I finished eating, I decided to call my friend Diana Clemente. She owned a car service that Cantor Fitzgerald used. Another coincidence? Fortunately, I was responsible for selecting the car company for Cantor. I negotiated directly with Diana, which was how we became good friends. I didn't have her direct number on me, but I remembered the main number.

"Big Apple Car, how can I help you?"

"Diana Clemente, please?"

"Just a moment."

"Diana Clemente, can I help you?"

"Diana? It's Ari Schonbrun," I said.

She immediately started to cry. "Oh my God, Ari. I thought you were dead."

After she regained her composure, I asked her if she could help me out. "Diana, they've shut the city down, and there's nothing going in or out. If I can get out to Queens, can you send a car to get me and take me back to my house?"

"Of course," she answered. "Here's a phone number. Call it anytime and they will give you whatever you need. I'm so happy that you are alive."

I thanked her and hung up.

I then called my brother, Ellie, at his office in midtown.

We discussed our options. Should he come down to me and then we'd walked over the Brooklyn Bridge, or should I go up to his office, so that we could walk over the Fifty-ninth Street Bridge? I told him that I wanted him to come down to me. He wanted to know why.

"Listen Ellie, we just had a terrorist attack and they're saying it's not over. You work in the diamond district. Lots and lots of Jews, right? If they're going to attack again what would be a logical target? Why don't you just come down here, and we'll walk across the Brooklyn Bridge."

"Listen," he said to me. "My office is below ground. We have a vault that is bomb proof. If anything happens, I'm in the vault. I am not going anywhere."

"Okay, you win," I said. "I'll come up to you. But listen, whatever you do, don't leave until I get there. Once I hang up and leave here, I won't be able to get in touch with you."

He assured me that he would wait, so I told him that I'd get there soon and hung up the phone. I went to the receptionist and let her know that I would be leaving.

"Do me a favor. If anybody calls looking for me, please let them know that I went to my brother's office."

I gave her his number, and then I left.

ARI SCHONBRUN

CHAPTER 11

Once back on the street, I decided I would walk across town to Sixth Avenue, then head north. When I got to Sixth Avenue, the entire scene was beyond surreal. It was like a snow day but without the snow. There wasn't a car in sight. The street was completely empty. And the sun still shone as brilliantly as it had early that morning. Another eerie *Twilight Zone* moment. As I walked on, I noticed people sitting in outdoor cafes and restaurants, and they were eating and laughing. I seethed with anger. I had just gone through hell, and here were these people acting as if nothing had happened. I wanted to scream. But I didn't. Instead, I just held it inside.

When I reached Twentieth Street, I saw a pay phone and decided to stop to call Ellie—just to let him know my progress. I put a quarter in and dialed, but the call didn't go through. I remember thinking to myself, "Great, I lost my quarter." I had just one more quarter left in my pocket but decided I had to save it, just in case.

I walked a block, and all of a sudden an MTA bus drove by and stopped at the corner. I ran to it and fortunately was able to get on. I couldn't believe that a public bus was in service, and that it actually stopped close enough for me to get on. I boarded and took out my Metrocard to pay.

When the driver saw it, she looked at me and said, "Put that thing away, we're not charging today."

Wow!!! Has New York City changed or what? That was something that I never thought I'd hear on a New York City bus.

She then announced to all the passengers, "If anybody wants to get off the bus, just ring the bell. We're not making regular stops."

When we approached Forty-fifth Street, somebody

rang the bell; and though I needed to get off at Forty-seventh Street, I decided to hop off there so the driver wouldn't have to make additional stops. I then walked two blocks to my brother's office. When I got to his door, I rang the bell.

"Who is it?"

"It's Ari Schonbrun. I'm here to see Elliot."

"Just a minute."

A few seconds passed, and then I was buzzed inside. I opened the door and walked down the set of stairs to my brother's office on the lower level. I walked through a set of double glass doors, and just as I entered the room, I saw my little brother (although he's my "little" brother, he is 6'1", 230 lbs.) standing in front of me. For a brief moment, I hesitated, then I grabbed him, hugging him hard, and then I started to cry. He grabbed me, too, and hugged me just as hard, and then said, "Ari, calm down. It's going to be okay."

We must've stood there hugging each other and crying for five minutes. How many times that day had I uttered those exact same words to others, and yet, finally, somebody was telling me that everything was going to be okay? I had been strong the entire day. I needed to be strong and reassuring for Virginia and strong for myself. It was survival. But now there was finally somebody that I could lean on, and I just lost it.

Eventually, we regained our composure, and then people in his office started asking me all kinds of questions about what had happened and everything that I'd seen. I told them whatever I knew, but I didn't feel like talking for long. Ellie and I needed to make some decisions. We hadn't yet decided what we were going to do: Should we leave now to walk across the Fifty-ninth Street Bridge, or should we wait? We had heard there was actually limited subway service.

"Ellie, do you really want to go down into a tunnel now for a subway?" I asked.

"I'd rather do that than walk," he answered.

"How about this. Let's go out to the subway and see if anybody knows what the situation is," I suggested. He agreed, and we headed out.

As we reached the corner of Forty-seventh Street and Sixth Avenue, a cop was standing right near the subway entrance.

"Excuse me, do you know if the subways are running now?" I asked.

"I understand that there's limited E and F subway service," the cop replied.

Ellie and I decided to go down and take our chances. We were at the station for the F train that would take us into Queens. The F train arrived a few minutes later, but as we approached the next station at Fifth Avenue and Fifty-third Street, Ellie said to me, "Let's get off and switch to the E train. We can take that to Jamaica and then catch the Long Island Rail Road home."

I said to him, "No! We're on a train, and it will take us out of the city. Let's just get out of here, and then I can call my friend who will send a car to pick us up. Besides, Jamaica is going to be a zoo, and we don't even know if the Long Island Rail Road is running."

"Come on," he said to me. "Let's just get off here and wait for an E train."

As we pulled into the station and the doors opened, there was a woman waiting on the platform. So I asked her, "Excuse me, do you know if the E train is running?"

"Oh, yes," she said. "As a matter of fact, you just missed one."

Ellie and I got off and waited for another E train

to arrive. As the doors of the F train closed and the train pulled away, I realized that the woman was still on the platform. I turned to Ellie and said, " If she didn't get on the E train and she didn't get on the F train, and those are the only two trains that stop here, then what is she waiting for?" I was so paranoid that I honestly thought she might be a terrorist. So I said to Ellie, "Let's go down to the other end of the platform."

We headed down the platform to the other end and waited. An F train came, but we didn't get on. Another F train arrived, and I said to Ellie, "Let's get on."

"No, let's wait for an E," he said.

By the time the third F train approached the station, I said, "We're getting on and getting out of here."

And so we were finally on our way out of the city en route to Queens. We decided to get off at Union Turnpike, which was the station I always got off at whenever I visited my mother-in-law, Evelyn Scherzer. At least I would know where I was. When we walked out of the subway station to the street level, we were standing on Queens Boulevard and Union Turnpike.

The traffic was a total mess. I checked my phone.

Finally, I had a signal. So I called the number that Diana had given me and asked for a car to pick us up in front of my mother-in-law's apartment building, which was just three blocks away from the subway station. I asked how long it would take and was told that the car should arrive within thirty minutes. When I looked at the traffic, I knew that there was no way the car would reach us within thirty minutes. And though I felt like arguing, I simply thanked the woman and hung up the phone.

Ellie then called his wife, Renee, and told her to meet us at my house. Then we walked the three long blocks to my mother-in-law's apartment, and when we were downstairs, I called her and explained to her that I didn't want to come up because I didn't want to take a chance of missing the car. She understood. A few minutes later, she came down, carrying a pitcher of water and two glasses for us. She was so great. She loved me like a son, and I loved her as if she were my own mother. When I was dating Joyce, I'd stop by her apartment on my way home from work, often when Joyce hadn't yet arrived home. Many a night she'd make dinner for me. Joyce used to complain that I was given steak while she got only a salad and leftovers. Evelyn passed away in the spring of 2010, and I miss her terribly.

After my mother-in-law went back upstairs, I decided to try to call my parents. It was about 4:30 p.m., which meant that it was 11:30 p.m. in Israel. When the phone started to ring, my heart actually began to pound in my chest, heavy with anticipation that I'd finally get to speak to my parents.

"Hello," my father answered.

"Hello Dad. It's Ari." And with those simple words he started to cry.

"Dad, why are you crying? I am alive! And not only that, I know that you know that I am alive because Avivit spoke to Renee from Belgium, and Renee told her I was alive and then Avivit called you from Belgium to tell you I was alive! So you knew I was okay! What's the matter, didn't you believe her?"

"No," he said to me. "I didn't believe anybody. As a matter of fact, I wasn't going to sleep tonight until I heard your voice."

I felt so happy that I had decided to call him then, and not wait until the next morning. He would've been up an entire night waiting on my call—waiting to be able to believe that I was alive. We spoke for a while. I answered his questions about what had happened and what I saw. He asked if my boss was alive. I had no idea. He asked if the company could go on, if I was still going to have a job. I told him I honestly had no idea, but I promised that I would keep him posted. I told him that I loved him and hung up the phone.

The car soon arrived after I finished speaking to him. Ellie and I climbed into the car, and then I called Joyce to let her know that we were in the car and on our way home. We finally arrived at my house around 5:30 p.m., and when I walked through the front door and into my home, there were twenty people in my living room. And I had no less than a hundred voice messages on my answering machine. That day I learned something very important. You actually have no idea how many friends you really do have until they all think that you are dead.

after

CHAPTER 12

The rest of that day is somewhat a blur. I remember going to shul (synagogue), which was around the corner from my house for Mincha (afternoon services). This was something that I did every day, albeit near my office. My sister came to my house but I was already in shul. Realizing her disappointment, Joyce offered to drive her to the shul. When they got there we were in the middle of Mincha so Joyce went to the door and asked one of the men to call me out.

"Oh my God Ari, are you okay?" she asked.

"I'm fine," I reassured her.

"You know, you've been through something really traumatic. Perhaps you should see someone to talk to."

Little did I know that I would have to hear that suggestion from many, many people for a very long time.

"I'm fine, really," I said, trying to sound assuring. We hugged and went back into shul.

Of course, everybody wanted to know what happened. It wouldn't be the last time that I'd tell the story. I found out later that my friend Curtis Grosser had called the Rebbe after he heard what had happened and was crying when he said, "Rebbe, Ari Schonbrun works in the Trade Center. Does anybody know if he's alive?" The Rebbe had called my wife, and she told him that I was alive and was walking down the stairs. Joyce had kept him posted as much as she could throughout the day.

When I returned home, I quickly discovered what this day had been like for my kids. As soon as it had become clear just how serious the situation was, the schools had decided to close. All of the students were sent home, although the school wouldn't let any child off the bus unless there was an adult there to meet them. Luckily, Joyce worked only two miles away from home, so she knew she could be there in time to meet our kids. My two boys, Baruch and Avrumi, were eight and six, respectively, and they couldn't quite comprehend the severity of what had occurred that day. Of course, they asked Joyce what had happened, but all she could do was reassure them that I was fine, trying her best to explain as best she could. When Rikki, my thirteen-year-old daughter, came home, she was aware that something terrible had happened, but she didn't have much information. The schools that day had been very careful about what the students were told.

"Mommy, I heard something happened to the World Trade Center. Is Daddy okay?"

"Daddy is fine. I spoke to him and he's trying to get home."

"What happened?" Rikki asked.

"There were two jet planes that went into the Trade Center, and both towers collapsed."

"Oh my God!!" Rikki shrieked. "What happened to Daddy? Is he really okay?"

"Yes, I told you Daddy is fine, and he's on his way home now."

"Thank God," Rikki said. And with that she started to go upstairs to her room. All of a sudden she stopped, turned to Joyce and said, "Oh my God, what happened to all of the stores?"

Joyce started to crack up, laughing hysterically. Even at thirteen, Rikki was already a shopaholic. She epitomized the "shop till you drop" personality. As soon as she knew that I was okay, the next more important thing, of course, were the stores in the Trade Center.

My oldest daughter, Chani, was fifteen at the time, and she always saw things in black and white. There were no shades of gray. And everything she did was always calculated. That's just the way her mind worked. She'd been sitting in class that morning when the second period teacher came into the classroom later than usual and looked more than just a little distraught.

"Girls, the World Trade Center was attacked. Two jetliners crashed into the buildings and the towers collapsed."

One of Chani's friends, who was sitting next to her right, turned to her and whispered, "Oh my God, Chani, doesn't your father work in the World Trade Center?" With that said, her friend sitting to the left of her shouted, "Oh my God, Chani, doesn't your father work in the World Trade Center?!"

The teacher, who obviously wasn't aware of this, turned to Chani and said, "Oh Chani! Your father works in the World Trade Center?! Do you want to call somebody?"

Very calmly, Chani turned to the teacher and said, "If my father is dead, he is not going to pick up the phone. If my mother hasn't heard this yet, I don't want to be the one to tell her. So who exactly would you like me to call?"

Needless to say, the teacher was in utter shock. Ultimately, she convinced Chani to call Joyce, and of course, Joyce had heard the news and they both started to cry.

Later that night around 11:30, after the house had calmed down, Joyce turned to me and said, "Are you getting paid on Friday? Do you need to look for a new job?"

I looked at her directly in the eye and said, "I don't know if I am getting paid on Friday. I do know though, if Howard Lutnick is dead, I need to look for a new job, but if he is alive, then we are going to be fine."

I don't think truer words were ever spoken.

It was only because of Howard's determination and commitment to the company that Cantor Fitzgerald survived, and now, ten years later, the firm is bigger, better and far stronger than it ever had been. The company was Howard's sole focus. He immediately made a promise to the families of the victims that the company would donate 25 percent of its profits to them for five years. And Howard knew in order to fulfill that promise the company was going to have to not only survive but become more profitable than it was before. He created the Cantor Relief Fund with a million dollar donation. He also vowed to pay the medical benefits of the victims' families for ten years. In addition, he vowed that the Cantor Relief Fund would exist until the last child born to the families graduated from college. To date, Cantor has paid out to the families over $180,000,000. The level of compassion and commitment to doing the right thing by all of the company's families affected by 9/11 remains unrivaled. No other company comes even close to Cantor.

CHAPTER 13

At about 3:30 a.m. that morning, my phone suddenly rang. It didn't wake me up because I couldn't fall asleep, but the phone's ring startled my wife.

"Hello?"

"Hello, is Ari Schonbrun there?"

"Who's calling?"

"I'm calling from Israel radio. Is this Ari?"

Joyce now more than a little frightened by the middle of the night call asked, "Who is it? Where are they calling from? How do you know they're not terrorists?" Looking back, this made absolutely no sense, but given what had happened that day, we were both paranoid. She was scared, and I must admit I was, too. After all, it was 3:30 in the morning.

"This is Ari, how did you get my number?"

"We got it from your mother in Israel."

"How did you get to my mother?"

"Somebody from the radio station knows her and called her."

"What do you want?"

"First of all, do you speak Hebrew?"

"Yes."

The conversation continued in Hebrew.

"Is it true that you were in the Twin Towers yesterday?"

"Yes."

"We would like to interview you on our radio program. Can we call you back at 6 a.m. New York time?"

"I'm sorry but at six o'clock I'm going to be in shul."

"Okay, how about 5:30?"

"Sure, why not."

"Okay, we will call you back at 5:30."

And then the phone went dead.

Joyce started yelling at me, "How do you know

they weren't terrorists?"

"I'll call my mother and ask her if she gave these guys my phone number."

So I called my mother, and she was more than a little surprised to hear from me considering it was so early in the morning.

"Hi, Ma?"

"Yes?"

"It's Ari."

"Ari? What are you doing awake at 3:45 in the morning?"

"Ma, did you give my number to a radio station?"

"Yes, I did."

"How did they get to you?"

"Sheila Harris has a nephew who works for a radio station, and he called her and asked if she knows anybody who worked in the Twin Towers who spoke Hebrew. She told him that she didn't, but 'why don't you call Sara Schonbrun. I think her son worked in the Trade Center, and he speaks Hebrew.' So he called, and asked if he could call you. I gave him your number but I told him not to call you now because it was 3:30 a.m. in New York. I told him to wait until later in the morning in New York."

"Ma, the guy is sitting on a scoop, did you really think he was going to wait?"

"I'm sorry."

"Forget about it. Anyway, they are going to call in another hour and a half, so listen to the radio if you want to hear the interview." Little did I realize that this was going to lead to a whole new career.

At 5:30 a.m., the phone rang and sure enough it was the radio station. I did a quick interview and then went to shul.

On September 12, 2001, everybody in my family went about their normal business—except for me. My kids went to school, my wife went to work, and I hung out at home. I had nowhere to go, and really nothing to do. It was actually a horrible feeling. Even worse, I had awakened that day with an odd smoky taste in my mouth and was a little nervous about it, so I called my doctor to make an appointment so he could check me out.

When I called and asked his nurse for an appointment, she asked me if the following Tuesday would be good for me.

"Listen, lady, I was in the Trade Center yesterday. I have a smoky taste in my mouth, and I'm worried that my lungs might be burned. I need to see the doctor ASAP."

She placed me on hold for a minute and then returned, "Can you be here by 11:00?"

After being examined, my doctor assured me that there was nothing wrong, that it was just smoke residue from the building and I had nothing to worry about. Thank God nothing was wrong. Of course, though, my doctor wanted to know the whole story. This was something I realized I'd have to get used to. Every time I met somebody who knew that I was in the Trade Center that day, I'd have to retell my story.

I returned home and for the rest of the day all I did was watch the same images over and over again on television: the planes going into the buildings, the buildings collapsing, the planes going into the building, the buildings collapsing... There were a few moments that day when I thought I might actually lose my mind.

Eventually, I called my boss and asked him what was going on. Were we working, and if so, where from? The company had set up a disaster recovery site in Rochelle Park, New Jersey, but he told me that space was incredibly tight and that I shouldn't bother coming in.

"John," I said. "You don't understand. I *need* to come to work. I can't stay at home another day."

"Okay, then," he said. "Come in tomorrow."

So I drove to Rochelle Park that Thursday, not knowing if it was even possible to get there by public transportation. When I arrived, it was an emotional reunion. It was the first that I had seen any of my coworkers since the attack. We all hugged, and we all cried. Then we got to work. We sat at folding tables and chairs, and shared phones; this was now our makeshift office.

I remember sitting with the people from accounting as we attempted to reconstruct balance sheets. Every time I'd call somebody, I would leave a call-back number but had to tell the person I likely wouldn't be the one who answered, so they'd need to ask for me. It was incredibly hectic, but we persevered because we had to get the company back on its feet.

After work, many of us went into Manhattan.

Cantor had taken a large ballroom in the Pierre Hotel, so that all of the families of the missing employees could gather and try to get and share information. Being there with all the families of missing employees was something that I will never forget. People carried posters of their missing family members, hugged each other, tried whatever they could to comfort each other, doing and saying whatever it took to give each other hope. Howard was there as well, talking to all of the families.

When Howard and I saw each other, we hugged. I had been in the ballroom for a while, helping however I could, talking to people, trying to give comfort, when all of a sudden, Stephen Merkel, who was the general counsel of the firm, asked me to step into another room. When I walked in I saw a large conference table, and seated around the table were all of the senior Cantor people who were still alive. In the middle of the table was a conference phone on speaker. On the other end of that phone was Lee Amaitis, who ran our London office. I remember thinking how amazing it was that he was on the phone because it was 9 p.m. New York time, which is 2 a.m. London time. We discussed strategy, in particular, how we were going to get the company back on its feet. At one point during the meeting, Howard got a call on his cell and excused himself. When he returned, he told us that Giuliani just called and told him that the city would do whatever it could to help us out. That was truly amazing. Howard then went around the table and gave instructions to each person. The meeting finally broke up at about 11 p.m. New York time, 4:00 a.m. London time.

On Friday, I drove out to the Rochelle Park office because there really wasn't any other way to get there, plus I was going to have to leave early for the Sabbath. Cantor owned numerous season tickets to all of the New York sports teams. I knew every seat for every team that Cantor owned because that had been part of my previous responsibilities. Yet, within the firm I didn't know if the people who now took care of the tickets were still alive, so I made it my business to call every New York sports team to let them know that if they had mailed our season tickets to our offices in the Trade Center those tickets were now buried in the rubble. And I told them that if they hadn't yet mailed them out, they'd have to hold them until I had an address for them to send them to.

It was stressful and difficult to manage because it was the end of the baseball season and the Yankees were going to the playoffs. On top of that, it was the start of the football season, as well as both preseason basketball and hockey. I was lucky that all of my old contacts were still around at the various sports teams and even more that they remembered me and acted upon my requests. Though it obviously seemed crazy to be concerned with ticket and attendance at games in the middle of the tragedy all around me, I was grateful to have this urgent task to sort out. Business had to go on, something Howard had made clear to us all.

By the time Monday arrived, we'd been given space by UBS in two locations: 299 Park Avenue for front-office personnel (traders and sales people) and Weehawken, New Jersey, for back-office staff. As part of the back office, Weehawken would now be my new home for the next nine months. So that Monday, a few us from Long Island decided to carpool, since we didn't have any idea how to get to Weehawken and definitely didn't know how to get there by train. That morning we ended up getting so lost that it took us over three hours to finally find the town. Eventually, the guys at UBS told us the best way to get there was by taking a train to Penn Station, followed by a bus to the pier on Thirty-fourth Street, and then a boat to cross the river. It turned out to be a brutal commute, especially during the winter months. I remember one morning before going to work my wife was telling me a story. I interrupted her and told her that I had to leave otherwise I was going to miss my train. And with that my son, Avrumi, who was six years old at the time said "aaand the bus aaand the boat". My wife and I both cracked up.

When we got set up in Weehawken, the people from UBS were incredibly nice and helpful. They obviously knew what we had been through and did everything they could to help us get settled, making sure we had all of the necessary supplies to conduct business. Their support helped make our lives feel somewhat normal. Even if it was just to make sure we had enough staplers, their efforts made us feel good.

During those first few weeks, it was difficult to

get any work done. All we could do was talk about who was known to be alive, who was considered missing and all who were known to have died. To this day, I still have the original list of the confirmed survivors from that first week. We became very close working together in Weehawken. The tragedy only served to deepen our bonds. We had lived and survived a nightmare. Now, we needed to rebuild our lives and our company together.

Before 9/11, Cantor had signed up for American Express' corporate card program. So one of my tasks in Weehawken was to gather all of the outstanding balances of every single cardholder and then figure out with HR who was still alive and what we were going to do about all of the balances for all of those employees who were no longer with us. The work was incredibly difficult for us all. Every day was a constant reminder of those we'd lost.

As a side note, it was four years later when American Express made, what I consider, an enormous faux pas. I was sitting at my desk and received a piece of mail from American Express. It was actually addressed to Keith Burns, who used to work for me and who was killed on 9/11. It was the renewal card for the purchasing card that they had pushed the firm to use for all of our purchasing, though we never did. And it was in Keith's name. You cannot imagine the memories that it brought back. I was so livid that I called American Express and gave them a piece of my mind. I actually spoke to the assistant of the CEO, making sure she knew how outraged I was that something like that could've happened. Especially after we had been so careful examining every single account just to make certain that something like this would never happen. I always knew how important it was to pay attention to details, but this mistake really drove it home.

There was a bar on the ground floor of the building in Weehawken that we used to go to every so often after work just to try to keep our sanity. We had several employees that came to Weehawken the Monday following 9/11 and within two weeks just disappeared and never came back. Some of them went to work at other firms, and some of them left the workforce entirely just to be with their families. Those of us who stayed formed bonds that never will be broken.

By June, we'd found new space in midtown Manhattan that could accommodate all the Cantor Fitzgerald employees, both front-office and back-office personnel. Once we got settled in our new office, life became a little more normal. At least I had returned to commuting via train and subway. Unfortunately, the new space wasn't ideal. The air conditioning didn't work in the summer, heat didn't work in the winter, and space was rather tight. It was a difficult environment to work in, but we did our best and made it work. Finally, in March 2005, we moved to our new permanent headquarters on Fifty-ninth Street between Park Avenue and Lexington Avenue, occupying the 2nd through the 7th floors. Our CEO vowed that Cantor would never go to a high floor again. That decision was very humbling for me. Where, prior to 9/11, we had been literally on top of the world, 105 stories in the air, where I had felt invincible, now we were at the bottom, working on the lowest floors possible.

ARI SCHONBRUN

CHAPTER 14

Virginia and I became incredibly close in the months and years after our near-death ordeal. I remember returning home from work one day and my wife said that I had received a package, but that she didn't recognize the name of the sender. I opened the package and inside was a beautiful knitted vest. There was a note of thanks. It was a gift from Virginia's mother. When I called her up to thank her, she couldn't stop thanking *me*. She only wanted to know if it fit because if it didn't, she wanted to knit me a new one.

Virginia has a house on the Jersey shore, and every

summer she invites me and my family to come visit her down there. Over the years, I've invited her to my daughter's wedding and to both of my son's Bar Mitzvahs, but unfortunately because of what she was going through, both physically and psychologically, she was unable to attend. She's promised me that she will be there to see my second daughter get married.

There's a great deal more that I could obviously say about what she and I went through, but none of that is important. All that matters is that our experience has strengthened and reaffirmed my belief that there is, without a doubt, a God who is running the world. Only He could take two people who utterly despised each other and turn them into the best of friends. I owe so much to Virginia. All I can say, as I do most every day, is God bless you, Virginia—both you and your mom.

My life has obviously changed since 9/11. In some ways, it's a completely new life. My sister-in-law, Yisraela, calls me every year on September 11 to wish me a happy birthday. My actual birthday is June 3, but as far as she is concerned, September 11 is my new birthday. She understands what most people don't or can't. I truly was given a new lease on life, a real second chance. But I wasn't the only one.

Dave worked at Cantor Fitzgerald on the 105th floor. He had told his customers the week before that if they wished to come up and visit, that Tuesday, September 11th, would be the best day. He reminded them that they must bring picture ID in order to get upstairs to his office. If they didn't have photo ID, security in the lobby would not let them up. On Monday, when he confirmed with them that they were coming, he again reminded them that they needed picture ID. So when they arrived on Tuesday morning at the Trade Center, they of course forgot to bring photo ID. Security wouldn't let them up, and instead called upstairs to Dave to let him know that he had guests downstairs. Dave's assistant took the call and was told that somebody would have to come down and get them. The assistant, who was eight months pregnant, offered to go but Dave wouldn't hear of it. Instead, he went down to the lobby to bring them up. When he arrived to greet them, the plane hit. His thoughtful gesture ended up saving his own life.

Tragically, his assistant did not survive. As he was standing in the lobby, a fireball came shooting out of one of the large elevators. Our coworker Lauren Manning happened to have been in the lobby waiting to go upstairs to her office. She had been standing about thirty feet in front of him. When he saw the fireball coming at him he was sure he was going to die. All of a sudden, the fire engulfed Lauren and just stopped. Dave could not believe how his life had been spared twice.

It was Monday morning, September 10, and Chris, who worked for Cantor Fitzgerald's public company eSpeed, was at his desk when the phone rang. His customer's eSpeed screens had just gone down, and he needed to get them back up and working as soon as possible. Chris said that it wouldn't be a problem and that he could actually walk him through the process over the phone; there was no need for him to go the customer's office. So he walked his customer through the steps to fix the issue and everything was fine. The following day, Tuesday, September 11, Chris again received a call from the customer with the same problem. Chris told him that he'd walk him through it again over the phone. This time the customer was upset: "Nothing is working. You get your ass down here now and you fix this once and for all." So Chris immediately left the office to help the customer with the problem. It was 8:30 a.m. Little did Chris realize it then, but his irate customer would actually save his life.

Unfortunately, there are also the people in the exact opposite situation: those who would normally have no reason to be in the World Trade Center but who just so happened to be there that day.

Cantor Fitzgerald, as a firm, banked with Chase. They also offered very favorable terms to its employees, so many of them banked there, as well. Citibank had been trying to win the account for years, but to no avail. Finally, Citibank was told that although Cantor wasn't going to switch its account, they would allow Citibank to come up to their offices and pitch its services to employees. Citibank was excited about the prospect of pitching to the company's approximately

1,000 employees, so they put together a very nice presentation. When that day finally arrived, they came to the Cantor offices promptly at 8:00 a.m. and set up shop to talk to employees. That day was Tuesday, September 11th. None of them survived.

Nancy was a single woman, 33 years old, who worked for our corporate travel agency, and she was just absolutely terrific. So terrific, in fact, that at the end of 2000, the head of our equities division asked her if she would like to come and work for him as his personal assistant. The money was much better, and the hours were pretty much the same. The only difference was that she had to be in the office by 7 a.m., but she didn't at all mind. She jumped at the opportunity and couldn't have been happier with her new job. She and I were very good friends. I even tried to set her up a few times. Sadly, she was in the office that day at 7 a.m. I met her family at the Pierre Hotel on Thursday, September 13, and tried to give them some comfort. They were a wonderful family. Much of the compensation that they received from the government was donated to charity. They actually donated an ambulance to Hatzalah and published a book of letters that were written to them by many of Nancy's friends after 9/11.

Ever since that day, the question continued to plague me: Why? Why did I survive in such a dramatic way, when thousands died around me? As an Orthodox Jew, my belief system simply doesn't relegate extraordinary events to just "coincidence." And I knew it *wasn't* just luck or coincidence. In fact, immediately after 9/11, many people came up to me and said, "There is a reason why you survived. You have a mission." No one seemed to have any thoughts on what my mission was, though. But I remember thinking to myself that if somebody would only tell me what my mission was, I would go out and do it, and then move on with my life.

Shortly after 9/11, I began to make certain that I always hugged and kissed my wife, along with each one of my kids, before I went to work because the thought that always raced through my mind was, "This might be the last time I ever see them." It took years for those daily thoughts to disappear. One thought, though, that never went away was: "*9/11 was a tragedy but if we don't learn something from it, it is twice the tragedy.*"

As the years have passed, I think I am beginning to understand why I was saved. Over the course of these years, I have spoken to audiences around the world about my experience. I tell them the story, and I focus on the hand of God. I remind them that it is not a coincidence. And when I finish speaking, inevitably, I am always approached by at least one individual, if not more, and am told that I have actually changed their lives.

How would you feel if somebody came up to you and said, "You know, you changed my life." To be told such a thing just once in your life is an amazing thing in and of itself, yet I hear such powerful statements every time I speak. Perhaps that is part of the reason I was saved. To be a witness. Sharing my story with others is one thing; truly learning from it is quite another.

The following anonymous poem says it better than I can ever hope to. The title of the poem is "If I Knew":

If I knew it would be the last time
that I'd see you fall asleep,
I would tuck you in more tightly and
pray the Lord, your soul to keep.

If I knew it would be the last time
that I see you walk out the door,
I would give you a hug and kiss and
call you back for one more.

If I knew it would be the last time I'd
hear your voice lifted up in praise,
I would videotape each action and word,
so I could play them back day after day.

If I knew it would be the last time,
to stop and say, "I love you,"
I would spare an extra minute instead
of assuming you would know *I do.*

If I knew it would be the last time I
would be there to share your day,
Well I'm sure you'll have many more,
so I can let just this one slip away.

For surely there's always tomorrow
to make up for an oversight,
And we always get a second chance
to make everything just right.

There will always be another
day to say, "I love you,"
And certainly there's another chance
to say our "Anything I can do?"

But just in case I might be wrong,
and today is all I get,
I'd like to say how much I love
and I hope we never forget.

Tomorrow is never promised to
anyone, young or old alike,
And today may be the last chance you
get to hold your loved one tight.

So if you're waiting for tomorrow,
why not do it today?
For if tomorrow never comes,

ARI SCHONBRUN

you'll surely regret the day,
That you didn't take that extra time
for a smile, a hug, or a kiss
And you were too busy to grant someone,
what turned out to be their one last wish.

So hold your loved ones close today,
and whisper in their ear,
Tell them how much you love them and
that you'll always hold them dear.

Take time to say, "I'm sorry," "Please
forgive me," "Thank you," "It's okay."
And if tomorrow never comes, you'll
have no regrets about today.

I was transformed by what happened on 9/11 from the inside out. Like most people in our country, what happened altered the way that I see the world and the times we are living in. But more personally, I don't see my life the same way and can no longer live it the same way I once did. I spent my entire career on Wall Street, where the motto each day is greed. The

World Trade Center said to the world, "Look at us. We are big. We are powerful. We are the epitome of capitalism." Of course, our accomplishments creating financial wealth have been impressive on a global scale. The free market, and the vision and achievement it represents, is amazing. Yet, the Wall Street culture, as I began to see it, warped people. Wall Street is full of multi-millionaires, and yet they're at their desks every day by 7 a.m. Why? Because they can't really live; they cannot relax; they are slaves to their greed. The bigger house. The nicer car. The grander vacation. That is all they care about. That is what life is all about in that greed-driven world. *And I was guilty of the exact same thing…* until that Tuesday.

I used to have one basic response to whatever my kids asked of me if it ever involved me giving them my time, "Daddy's got to work."

They would ask, "Daddy, can you come to the school play? I've got the lead role."

"Sorry, Daddy's got to work."

"Daddy, can you come on a class trip? We're going to the zoo."

"Sorry, Daddy's got to work."

"Daddy, can you come to mock trial? I'm the lead attorney and it's after school so it's after work. You can come, right?"

"Sorry, Daddy's got to work late."

Daddy's got to work. Daddy's got to work. Daddy's got to work. That was my constant refrain... Until that Tuesday.

Today, Daddy's at the school plays; Daddy's on the class trips; Daddy is wherever his children need him to be because that's what is most important in life.

My work will always be there, but the unique things my kids are going to go through in life, they will only go through once. And I want to make sure that I'm part of all their experiences. I want to be part of their life for my own sake but also on behalf of all the daddies that did not come home on 9/11 and will never have the chance to do the same. My renewed commitment to being a father has been the core personal change that happened to me, but believe it or not there is more.

In 1990, after having our two beautiful girls, my wife was again pregnant. She was six weeks along when she started to experience severe abdominal pain and went to the doctor for a check-up. He sent her to the hospital for a sonogram and found a cyst the size of a melon on one of her ovaries. He told her that he needed to operate right away. It was a Friday afternoon, and my wife hadn't finished all of her preparations for the Sabbath, so she told the doctor that she must go home and that she'd be back on Sunday. He told her that if she went home there was a very good chance that she would be back on Sunday but most likely in box. He took her straight to the operating room and successfully removed the cyst while saving the ovary.

Unfortunately, he had to terminate the pregnancy. We were happy that her life had been saved, but we were sad over the loss of the fetus. The way we looked at it, however, it wasn't the end of the world. Two years later we had our third child, a boy, and then three years after that we had our fourth child, also another boy. In 1995, after our fourth child was born, the doctors told Joyce that she wouldn't be able to have any more children. Joyce and I were not overly upset because we already had four beautiful children and felt very blessed. Fast forward eight years, it's now

2003 and Joyce wasn't feeling well, so she went to the doctor. He told her that she had something called a blighted ovum and that she would need a D and C.

I was scheduled to fly to London on a business trip, and then from London to Israel to visit my parents for the weekend. I told Joyce that I was going to postpone the trip until after her procedure, but she assured me that it was only a minor procedure and that there wasn't any need for me to stay. I agreed on the condition that she call me right after the procedure.

It was Thursday afternoon in London, and she told me that she was going to have the procedure either later that day or Friday morning. Since I was going to be getting on a plane that day, I told her to call me Friday morning New York time, which would be the afternoon in Israel. About thirty minutes before the Sabbath in Israel, my parent's house phone rang. It was Joyce. I got on the phone and asked her how it went.

"They found a heartbeat," Joyce said to me.

"Huh? What? What are you talking about?"

"I'm pregnant," she said.

I was in total shock. "How is that possible? The doctors said that you couldn't have any more kids?"

"I guess they were wrong."

When I got home, Joyce and I decided that we needed to tell the kids. We waited until Friday night when we were sitting altogether at the Shabbos meal.

"Kids, mommy and I decided that this year, instead of giving a lot of little gifts for Chanukah we are going to get one big family gift."

"We're getting a dog?" they asked excitedly

"Not exactly," I said.

Just then it sunk in. Chani and Rikki looked at us and said "Oh no! Are you kidding? You mean…?"

"Yup"

"What's wrong with you people? What, do you need a chaperone?"

Yoni came into the world that December 2003, our fifth child, and third boy. When we called the house to tell the kids that they had a new brother, Avrumi yelled "Yes, we won." It was now three boys against two girls. Yoni turned our world upside down. We had thought those child-rearing days were behind us, but he's a true blessing. I firmly believe that the soul that was lost in 1990 due to the ovarian cyst was a soul that needed to enter this world, but it just wasn't the right time. Eight and a half years later was the time. So, perhaps that was another reason I was saved. There were apparently still miracles happening in my life. And, there was purpose. I knew deep down in my heart that my life had still more purpose, but it was left for me to figure out what that would be.

As I began to speak more often, sharing my story with more people, affecting more and more lives, I realized that there *was* more. But it wasn't actually bigger, rather it was smaller and simpler, as you will see below.

There's a story about a group of students that were asked to list what they thought were the present Seven Wonders of the World. Though there was some disagreement among the students, the following received the most votes:

Egypt's Great Pyramids
Taj Mahal
Grand Canyon
Panama Canal
Empire State Building
St. Peter's Basilica
China's Great Wall

As the teacher gathered the votes, she noticed that one quiet student hadn't turned in her paper. So she asked the girl if she was having trouble with her list.

The girl replied, "Yes, a little. I couldn't quite make up my mind because there were so many."

"Well, tell us what you have, and maybe we can help," the teacher said.

The girl hesitated, then read from her paper, "I think the seven wonders of the world are: to touch, to taste, to see, to hear." She hesitated a little, then added: "to feel, to laugh, and to love."

The room was absolutely silent. Those things we overlook as simple and "ordinary" are truly wondrous.

CHAPTER 15

Do you remember the blackout in August of 2003? The entire northeast corridor of the United States was affected. Fifty million people lost power. I remember I was sitting at my desk at about four that afternoon when the lights suddenly went out and my computer went dead. Joyce was on the Long Island Railroad. She immediately called me to ask what it means if the train stops moving in the middle of stations for no apparent reason. My wife rarely, if ever, took the train because she worked just two miles from our home and never had a reason to go into the city. Yet on this day she had to go into the city to attend a conference. As a non-commuter she was not at all familiar with the day-to-day workings of the railroad, so when it suddenly stopped she thought it was a normal occurrence and simply wanted to know what it meant.

The first thing that went through my mind was "terrorist attack." The people in my office were kidding around about it, but I was scared out of my mind. When I raised the possibility that it could be an attack, they immediately became somber. Fortunately, it wasn't, just a freak accident that put 50 million in the dark; though deep down, I still believe it was a terrorist attack that was covered up so the country wouldn't be alarmed.

I remember thinking, "What's the point?"

The only thing that made sense to me was that God was sending us a message. He was telling us, "People, you are in such a state of spiritual darkness and you don't even know it. How can I make you understand?" And so he put 50 million people into darkness, as if to say, "This is the spiritual darkness that you are in. You need to wake up and change."

Did we listen? No. So what did he do next? He

hit us in our wallets. He brought the economic meltdown, putting millions of people out of work. He threw the entire world into an overnight recession. No easy feat, unless you're God. Did we learn from that? No. So he brought along Bernie Madoff to represent the very worst part of our greed-driven world by hitting the highest net worth individuals and the widows and elderly who gave him their life savings. And he hit schools, synagogues and charities.

Let us not forget the natural disasters. The earthquake in Japan and the subsequent tsunami in March of 2011. Tens of thousands of people were killed. The tornadoes that have hit the United States in 2011 were in record number, causing billions of dollars in damage and taking countless lives. Does anybody see a pattern here? *We need to make a change.*

We live during a time that too closely resembles the end of the great Roman and Greek empires. We are losing our way as a culture, and we have to re-examine what is truly most important to us. The behavior I see around me, the ridiculous and adolescent antics of so-called adults, is beyond embarrassing. Today, anything goes. From extramarital affairs to sending out naked pictures of yourself on cell phones. (Thank you Brett Favre and Andrew Weiner.) It's no longer even shocking; it's almost expected.

Despite all of this degrading and shameful behavior, oddly, it's the idea of religion, of serving a Creator, that embarrasses so many people. How laughable. Mentioning God in a public school or public square is considered threatening or in poor taste. I consider myself lucky that I don't have this problem. Being raised an Orthodox Jew, I had a head start organizing my daily life around God. Unlike the majority of people, I have always taken daily actions—prayer, Torah study, keeping kosher, wearing a yarmulke— that have helped to reinforce and renew my commitment to God. But despite my daily rituals built around my devotion to God, there were times when I lost sight of what was really important. Was I truly aware of what I was doing through all of these practices, or was I just going through the motions most of the time? Did I just do the minimum that was required and find convenient excuses not to attend one more study session or concentrate more on the words of my prayers? September 11, 2001, was a day of reckoning for me. I had to figure out how I was making use of my life.

I needed to make a change. Yet, it took a group of terrorists flying a plane into a building, causing an inferno and ultimately two buildings to collapse—that for but the grace of God did not collapse on me—to force me to make a change. And change I did. I started paying more attention to my prayers, understanding what I was saying and not just mumbling the words. Prior to 9/11, I used to study the Talmud one hour a week. One hour a week?? Well, of course, I didn't have more than an hour a week. After all, I was a basketball fan, a football fan, and a baseball fan, and I hated whenever I missed my teams play. I had sports on the television all of the time. And of course there were my favorite TV shows that I couldn't miss. And what about my favorite movie channels? I couldn't miss any of those. Are you kidding me?? But once I shut off the TV, I realized I had all kinds of time. Now I use that time to study both the Bible and the Talmud.

But understand something and this is very important; the changes I made did not happen overnight.

I was the same guy on Wednesday, September 12, 2001, that I'd been on Tuesday, September 11, 2001; the only difference being that I had lost 658 friends and coworkers. I didn't say to myself, "Oh my God, what a miracle. I am going to change my whole life. I am going to become a Rabbi or a mystic, and isolate myself on the top of the mountain and get closer to God." No, it took many months until it finally sunk in, until it finally began to reverberate inside me, awakening me to the miracles that happened to me on that fateful day. And because it took so long, the change that happened within me stuck. I remember that the city of New York changed the very next day. People became nicer. People had a feeling of unity. All for one and one for all. It was truly incredible! It barely lasted six months. Before we knew it, New York had reverted back to what it had been prior to 9/11 and became even worse. And this change back to the old ways was something that I witnessed even among those I worked with every day. At first, they changed for the better, but then six months later many had returned to their old selves. I was *not* going to let that happen to me. And it hasn't.

We need to make a change. Do you know what the definition of insanity is? Doing the same thing over and over again and expecting different results. Unless we do something different, nothing is going to change. As I sit here now, on the eve of the tenth anniversary of 9/11, the ways in which the United States is being pummeled, the crises we face on so many fronts, are only increasing. We are being shown that things can no longer go on as they were.

So what should we do?

How about first starting with personal change? The only thing we truly have any control over is our own actions. One action can cause a chain reaction. I lived through something that most of us could have never imagined. Just as the Titanic could never sink, and the Challenger could never explode at take-off, the Twin Towers could never fall down in a heap of paper, concrete and ash. But unimaginable things can happen, the Titanic *did* sink, the Challenger *did* blow up—and on that day, the Twin Towers *did* collapse. When your world is falling apart (literally), what voice do you listen to? Usually, the quick choices you make are the same kinds of choices you make on any other day. What moral imperative do you follow on any ordinary day? Do you rush past other people or do you help them? Do you look for answers or wait for others to give you instructions? Do you have faith in something beyond yourself, or do you give up and say it's all for nothing?

As simple as it seems, the best way to change the effects of such a major and horrific tragedy is not just to rebuild towers, but to rebuild ourselves, to make ourselves stronger and better, and have these changes cause a ripple effect that spreads to all those around us.

Take one thing that you are not doing today, that you could do to make yourself better, no matter how basic, and make the conscious decision to do better. Changing one character trait can be as hard as treating an addiction. In my life, one of my worst habits was cursing, so I decided to try to rid myself of that bad habit. I work on Wall Street. Do you have any idea the type of language that is spoken in the offices on Wall Street throughout the day? Some of these people are worse than drunken sailors. So I knew this was going to be a challenge. Yet, once I took it upon myself to make this change, it actually had an effect on the people who work with me. When colleagues are around my desk, they never curse because they know I don't. And if they do happen to curse, they now immediately apologize.

Most of us have some idea which character traits or behaviors we have that are less than attractive, that show us as less than who we should or want to be. And sometimes we pledge to ourselves that we'll begin to change those less desirable traits, but we usually say to ourselves, or others, that we'll get to it soon...one of these days... Those who died on 9/11 were every imaginable type of person—many fine, good; and some downright incredible. But every single one of them lost his or her chance to improve themselves, to change those things within their control that would make them and the world around them better. Many of us think often of how we'd like to show one more act of kindness, say one more prayer, take on the responsibility of making a loved one's life easier, or do one more act of charity. What are we waiting for? Now is the time to act.

All of us have heard the phrase "random acts of kindness." You don't really have to look very hard to find someone waiting to receive one of those random acts. There are times when people are going through a rough patch, and all they need is a kind word. This is such a simple yet marvelous thing to give, and it makes people feel entirely different. *Most people's problems are borne from not life itself but from their attitude toward life.* If they changed their attitude, their whole life would change. As I said earlier, right after 9/11, New York City had changed. Everybody in the city was united. Everybody was nicer to each other. It lasted exactly six months. After that, everybody went back to the way they were before. We need to remember what those six months felt like. More than ever, we are going to need each other even more in the times ahead.

Everybody can create good in the world, whether it's noticing who needs help in your personal life, or getting involved with an organization that helps others on a bigger scale. You can give money, time or help of any kind. There is an unlimited need for volunteers and organizations who need them. It doesn't really matter which positive change you choose to put into place. All that matters is if you pick one thing and stick to it, you will see and feel the change in you, and you will see how your actions can have positive effects on the people around you. You will also realize that you have more capacity to change than you think. After committing to one change or act of kindness, you will then take upon yourself one more thing and then you'll add something else, until before you realize it, you have changed your life for good.

But you have to start now. Don't wait until next week. Don't wait until after finals. Don't wait until the project at work is done. Don't wait until your child starts school because (as you tell yourself) *then* you will have more time. There are millions of excuses that people come up with for not starting something. So, start today. Commit to making a positive change in your life. Write down your resolution on a piece of paper and carry that paper in your pocket. Put it on your fridge or tape it to your computer screen or make a Post-It Note on your iPad or on your phone. Look at it every day, so that you never forget.

There are millions of excuses as to why people don't follow through on their commitments. There's a reason why gyms offer free or discounted membership for the first month if you sign up for a year. They know that this kind of promotion will bring in customers who, although initially gung-ho about getting fit, will eventually stop going. They peter out but keep paying the membership fees. They don't want to give up their membership because they tell themselves that they are going to start going again *next month*. There's a reason why there are so many diets on the market. People start and then soon stop. They blame the diet and then move on to the next one. It's always somebody else's fault. It's very difficult to admit to yourself that it is your own fault. Well now it is time to look yourself square in the eye and say" "If it is to be, it's up to me." Don't give up your resolution to make a personal change. Stick to it. They say that it takes thirty days to form a new habit. If you do the same thing over and over again for a month, it will ultimately become routine. Let today be the first day of your thirty days to positive change. Start now. I am begging you. Please don't wait and don't make excuses. And whatever you do, don't listen to the naysayers. There will always be plenty of people in your life who will give you a hundred reasons why you can't do something. These are the people that you need to stay away from. Avoid them, please. They are negative people. You may think they are your friends but if they are holding you back from making a positive change in your life, they are not true friends. You need to surround yourself with positive people. People who think like you do. People who are interested in making a change as well. These will be your true friends. These are the people you want to surround yourself with.

So, what should you do?

Find a larger foundation for your life. Learn more about your own religious traditions. They will give you an anchor to stay strong and remain positive during difficult times. Seek out good teachers, and the give-and-take of deep learning will add a new depth and dimension to your everyday life. If it is possible, be part of a community that shares your values, and you will be a lifeline for each other.

Most importantly, we have to wake up and realize that our world is so much bigger than our careers, our houses, our cars or even ourselves.

There is a story about a young and successful

executive who was traveling down a neighborhood street going a little too fast in his brand new shiny Jaguar. He was watching for kids darting out from between parked cars when he thought he saw something. As his car passed, no children appeared. Instead, a brick smashed the car's side door. He slammed on the brakes, put the car into reverse and backed up to where the brick had been thrown. The angry driver jumped out, grabbed the nearest kid and pushed him up against the car shouting, "What was that all about and who are you? Just what the heck are you doing? That's a new car and that brick you threw is going to cost me a lot of money. Why did you do it?"

The young boy apologetic, "Please mister...Please, I'm sorry. I didn't know what else to do. I threw the brick because no one else would stop." With tears streaming down his face and off his chin, the young boy pointed to a place just around a parked car.

"It's my brother. He rolled off the curb and fell out of his wheelchair and I can't lift him up." Sobbing uncontrollably, the boy then asked the stunned executive, "Would you please help me get him back into his wheelchair? He's hurt and he's too heavy for me."

Moved beyond words, the driver tried to swallow the lump in his throat. He lifted the handicapped boy back into the wheelchair, then took out his handkerchief and wiped at the fresh scrapes and cuts.

Shaken, the man simply watched the boy push his wheelchair-bound brother down the sidewalk toward home. It was a long, slow walk back to the Jaguar. The damage was noticeable, but the driver never repaired the dented side door. He kept the dent to remind him of this message: don't go through life so fast that someone has to throw a brick at you to get your attention.

God whispers to our souls and speaks to our hearts. The problem is that we are often so busy running through life we don't have time to listen. We are too busy with the material world, so we ignore the whispers. It is then that He has to throw a brick at us to wake us up: to tell us that we aren't doing the right things and that we need to make a change. Do you see a theme here? Now, I've had a brick thrown at me, so I know. But you. You have a choice. You can listen to the whisper…or you can wait for the brick.